# Loving the Difficult

"I life-guarded from three to five in the afternoon, seven days a week." With Yarah Hooley, one of the first learners in the pool.

# Jane Rule

# LOVING THE DIFFICULT

HEDGEROW PRESS • 2008

*Library and Archives Canada Cataloguing in Publication*
Rule, Jane, 1931–2007
Loving the Difficult / Jane Rule

ISBN 978-0-9736882-6-9
1. Rule, Jane, 1931-2007. 2. Authors, Canadian (English)—
20th century—Biography. I. Title.
PS8535.U77L68 2008    c814'.54    C2007-907404-9

Published by
Hedgerow Press
P.O. BOX 2471
Sidney, B.C. V8L 3Y3
hedgep@telus.net
www.hedgerowpress.com

Cover and text design: Frances Hunter
Cover photo: © IT Stock / Photolibrary
Photographs courtesy the Estate of Jane Rule

Printed and bound in Canada
on 100% post consumer recycled paper

*For You*

# CONTENTS

OTHER WORKS BY JANE RULE

*Desert of the Heart* (1964)

*This Is Not For You* (1970)

*Against the Season* (1971)

*Lesbian Images* (1975)

*Theme for Diverse Instruments* (1975)

*The Young in One Another's Arms* (1977)

*Contract With the World* (1980)

*Outlander* (1981)

*Inland Passage* (1985)

*A Hot-Eyed Moderate* (1985)

*Memory Board* (1987)

*After the Fire* (1989)

# LOVING THE DIFFICULT

{ November 2006 }

I have often tried to figure out why I, who as a child feared most reciting or reading aloud in class and any assigned long-term project, in my twenties found myself a teacher and writer of novels. Against all advice and encouragement, I did not love what I was naturally good at like math, which seemed to me an addiction to one right answer, dangerous to indulge and mainly beside the point. If I had had the career pressure my brother suffered, I would probably have become a chartered accountant. Or with my height and skill I might have been a professional basketball player or a coach, though I disliked and mistrusted competition which of necessity produces as many losers as winners, another misguided pursuit.

Ambition surely grows as much from defects as from talents. As a child, my fear of speaking in public was dwarfed by my fear of the dark, which so shamed me I could never admit it. I called for water, for extra blankets, but never asked for a night-light. One night, as the rain attacked the French doors in my bedroom and the wind shadowed frantically dancing trees against the walls, I could stand the terror no longer. I got up, dressed and walked out those French doors into the storm, walked and walked until, drenched and very cold but perfectly safe, I went home to bed and slept. At twenty-one, I spent a year writing a couple of pages of prose a day until the length of a novel held no more unreal terrors than a dark room at night. Throughout my teaching and lecturing life, I have had moments of stage fright, but I have learned that fear can either shake a voice or give it resonance, and the depth of my voice, for which I was teased as a child, has become an asset.

Of course, fear alone is not motivation enough. I've never tried to overcome my fear of heights. I avoid them as I do aggressive dogs. I don't want to be a mountain climber or pet owner.

I didn't have to be good at but I had to love what I did whether I feared it or not. Falling in love is not a group activity though it can happen in a crowded room. To stay in love is an act of profound privacy, as all learning is. Education's most grievous error is to confuse practice and performance, to force children to do what they don't know how to do in public, hour after hour, day after day, as if humiliation were the key to competence.

In my teens I often had a fantasy of going back to first grade and acing it. In high school I felt ready to turn first grade into a success, my penmanship under adequate control, given the limits of left-handedness, every word in the *Dick and Jane* reader happily, boringly familiar. In the first grade I had even failed nap, had had a chair put over my head to keep me from sitting up and looking around. I didn't get it that you could fake sleep, that nap was a performance which had nothing to do with real rest.

The harder lesson is to make a connection between practice and performance that is not a matter of faking it. Once in geometry class I went to the board to work out a proof by means not outlined in the book. When I had finished, I half expected a reprimand. "Beautiful," the teacher said. And I saw that it was.

I was more apt to fall in love with good teachers than with what they taught, though it took me a long time to make the distinction. I was not, after all, in love with geometry or, for that matter, Milton, but those teachers really were, and I found that I learned a lot from practicing even what I might never truly perform.

I came to writing by loving language I wanted to make my own. I came to teaching to create a climate for others to fall in love with the craft that can give voice to what matters most: to understand, challenge and celebrate what it is to be human. However hard it is, however frightening, however dubious the worldly rewards, I have lived my life doing what I want and love to do, practicing in private, performing in public, offering the gifts I have against the silencing odds.

# REFRAIN

{ September 2001 }

My friend Elisabeth Hopkins, who died at the age of ninety-seven, spent the last years of her life making new friends for whom the stories of her life could be fresh and surprising. I helped her in that enterprise, in part to be sure that I could hear those stories again and again, familiar and reassuring, sometimes newly thought-provoking. She learned not to apologize to me for having told a story before. Why, particularly as we grow older, do we fear repetition, when it is one of the more important tasks of old age? After Elisabeth died, friends discovered that she had been selective in her repetitions; stories familiar to some of us were unknown to others as if she had sensed who might benefit and who might misjudge or misuse certain of her life's experiences. We learned then something of what she thought of us as well as of herself in those last years of her life.

We are not all storytellers, and those of us who are have different and not always conscious motives. The oral traditions of our ancestors are lost to us. We are no longer required to hold and hand down our culture and history, which can be committed to paper instead. We don't even any longer require children to memorize dates or poems. Yet there is still a desire to know by heart what moves and matters to us. Children and adolescents without prompting learn the words and melodies of songs which, like all words to be sung, depend on repetition, as in the classic ballad refrain. People who have forgotten the narrative verses can usually join in for "Ol' Man River, he just keeps rollin' along." Just so in most families there are verbal refrains (in mine, "Anything that's worth doing is worth overdoing") which come from shared experience and affirm their clannish value. But we have no acknowledged place for the storytellers, in the family or the community, and only an uncertain grasp of the value of the stories themselves.

In such a climate, the storyteller also becomes uncertain. What could carry a life's experience and insight can, for an impatient or indifferent audience, deteriorate into a litany of complaint and disappointment from which everyone turns away. Those with any self-respect and self-control fall silent. But the needs both to speak and to listen remain.

"Once upon a time" is a signal not only of a promise to return to a particular time for a particular story but of a story heard before, perhaps many times before, and part of the deep pleasure is being able to anticipate not only events but details of language: "The sky is falling, Chicken Little." The listener is learning to become the teller.

But how do we learn to tell our own stories to an audience willing to listen? We have to begin and go on being willing listeners, to prompt our teachers to their own power. When I was a child, I learned to know my relatives by the stories they were willing to tell. I liked most those who would tell what it was like in 'olden times' when they were children themselves, my father and his twin brother punished for riding a pregnant sow, my grandmother singing because she was told not to talk in school, my mother taken to visit her nanny's lover. Their adventures and misadventures in childhood gave me a sense of kinship with them as well as a way of valuing my own experiences.

One of my grandmothers had a gift for making up stories. I could give her a single word, and it was all the prompting she needed to take me into magical forests, families of animals, haunted houses. She was the first to teach me that stories began in people's heads before they were written down in books.

I visited three great-uncles on their farm in Kentucky. Lucien slept most of the morning, read and wrote most of the night, but he could always be persuaded to tell family stories about his preacher father, who believed in hell but not in heaven and was forced to leave the church, about his saintly mother, the fire that burned down the first farmhouse, taking the life of a serving-girl and her illegitimate child. Wallace, because of that fire, preferred to sleep in a tent out in the backyard. He was a water witcher and lay preacher. His stories came from the Bible and were intended to scare goodness into sinners. Clarence got

"I chose to join my life with another independent woman... Helen Sonthoff."

up at dawn to milk the cows. His stories were practical, told with hands as well as words, as I learned to milk, shuck corn, clean chickens. But he also liked to tell me about the day he took a lady friend flying over Louisville for a whole hour.

If my grownups didn't repeat themselves without prompting, I encouraged them. "Tell again...." "Tell about when...." I was rarely shooed away. I was learning the lesson of getting attention by giving it wholeheartedly.

What impeded my own development as a teller of stories was a critical audience, made up of my mother and older brother. The stories that interested me were too often the sort improper to tell. What inspired me was either something exciting or something I didn't quite understand. Reporting excitement—"Arthur peed on the daffodils," "Arthur took the dimes on the dresser," "Arthur told Mrs. Dirkheimer to shut up"—came under the pejorative category of "Tattletale." What I didn't quite understand nearly always had to do with sex, and I rarely got any helpful explanations. Before I could launch myself as an acceptable storyteller, I first had to learn the categories of things that shouldn't be spoken at all, like anybody's peculiarities, like family secrets, like what anybody said about anybody else, like God and Jesus. I was rebuked for naming one doll Jesus, even though I gave him the preferred upper berth in my toy train sleeping car. The only meaning of the word "refrain" I learned until I studied poetry was, "Do not repeat."

"Stop me if you've heard this one" may be useful for tired jokes (though whoever really gets stopped?), but for real stories the admonition should be, "If you've heard this before, listen again more carefully. It may become one of your stories to tell."

In our time, family stories and stories of community may be different as so many of us move away from our geographic roots. I do tell family stories to people who have never known any of my relatives, sometimes because they are funny or shocking or insightful, but also as a way of being known. More and more, I collect island stories about this small community I've lived in for twenty-five years. Some are melodramatic: accidents, betrayals, deaths. Some have to do with local politics. The ones I like best are quieter, catch the flavor of island living. Here is one of those: George Griffiths walked into the post office with a cast on his arm. Jim Ripley, the postmaster, asked, "What happened to you, George?" "I heard I fell out of a tree," George replied. That's one I'll tell over and over again because it does place us so clearly, comically, and vulnerably in the narrative of our community. I'll be glad when I've told it often enough for some in my audience to sing out with me, "I heard I fell out of a tree."

# DECEPTIONS IN SEARCH
# OF THE TRUTH

{ 1990 }

Early in my writing life I wrote a story called "A Walk by Himself" about a boy in his first year at college, recorded it on tape and sent it to CBC's "Anthology." The story was rejected because the editors admitted a frank bias against autobiographical material. I was very angry both at such a bias and their assumption that the piece was autobiographical. I should probably have been flattered that the story was convincing enough to a staff of male editors for them to make that mistake. At the time, having the story accepted would have done more for my confidence.

Their error was also encouraged by the depth of my voice, a property I did not gain as boys do at puberty but have had since

I began to speak. I am always mistaken for a man on the phone, an embarrassment I have learned to turn to my advantage when I can. I have discovered that when I need advice I should pitch my voice unnaturally high, or my ignorance will be treated with impatience and even contempt. When I want to lodge a complaint, give advice or an order, I speak in my normal voice and receive a prompt, "Yes sir." But I still feel uncomfortably split when I am, say, making plane reservations for myself and get the question, "And where can she be reached?" I feel like my own doting father managing the hard details of the public world for me.

Over the years, by this means, I have learned a lot about socially constructed expectations of gender, how little they really have to do with who people are, what they are capable of and what they need. As a writer of fiction, my job is to understand as much as I can of social constructions of all sorts, the ways they inhibit, distort, and, to varying degrees, shape the much more complex and individual creatures who try to lead their own lives.

For women writers gender has been an issue not only inside our texts but on their covers. Even today in genres like the murder mystery women write under male pseudonyms, or with anonymous initials, in order to reach a male audience. A bookseller I knew delighted in offering men who asked specifically for male authors of mysteries women authors in those disguises. We still suffer from a large group of readers who automatically take us less seriously because of our gender. Fewer of us now go the route of George Eliot and most of us no longer take satirical swipes at our own craft, Jane Austen's defense. We are learning to take ourselves seriously, which is by definition a gender disturbance in women.

The issues of gender inside our texts seem to me both less important and more complex than recent debates about authenticity of voice might suggest. The vast majority of us have been marginalized by gender, class and/or race. Our first attempts to break our silence are bound to include defensive strategies. Most of my earliest stories were written from a male point of view because I wanted my characters to be taken seriously. They are not very convincing stories, not because I was incapable of writing from a male point of view but because I chose that point of view for the wrong reason. James Baldwin made his main character in *Giovanni's Room* self-consciously white as well as homosexual. The difficulty here is not Baldwin's inability to present the view of a white man but his need to assert that whiteness against the reader's assumption that Baldwin's characters will be black because he is. His choice of whiteness may also have come from defensiveness about his own homosexuality.

The choice of point of view should be dictated by the needs of the narrative, not by the assumptions of the audience or the defensiveness of the writer. Good writing does not serve cultural biases though it may often illuminate them. Good writing does not protect anyone, not even the writer.

There is no woman's point of view instantly recognizable as automatically female. In *My Name is Mary Dunne*, Brian Moore's main female character seems to me self-consciously preoccupied with her menstrual periods. I'm sure there are some women who are but that is not Moore's point. He simply wants to be sure she sounds like a woman. Both men and women

"Characters in fiction are not real people
any more than photographs are real people."

have written about women convincingly without concern for their menstrual cycles. On the far side of adolescence most people take their primary and secondary sexual characteristics for granted. Authenticity is about a thousand other things, all chosen for the insight they bring to a character.

It is a peculiarity of contemporary Canadian women writers that the vast majority are mothers. Our foremothers were mainly not mothers and therefore probably in the eyes of their society not successful examples of their sex. Even mothers don't automatically qualify. Most of ours are divorced. I myself am a lesbian. How can any one of us claim to speak for women, unless we are taken in by the deception of gender?

As writers, it is not our job to represent our sex, though in the course of our careers we will probably be called upon to create a number of female characters. If any one of them can be judged "typically female" we'll know in that instance we have failed to serve our own humanity unless, of course, we're writing farce.

The ability to create a range of characters is one of the requirements for a writer of fiction. Each of us draws on our own experience, sometimes quite directly, much more often by such circuitous and subterranean ways neither reader nor writer could uncover the connection. Authenticity cannot, therefore, be judged by the identity or experience of the writer. It can only be tested in the work itself.

I have been asked how I can write realistically about children when I have none of my own. I was a child. I have also spent more time with children than many people do because I like having them around for what they teach me not only about childhood but about language and politics.

I have been asked how I can write about old people when I'm not yet sixty myself. Like children, the old are not segregated in my mind or my life. My grandparents and even my great-grandparents were very real to me. I have always had close friends much older than I. I have also had arthritis since I was in my early forties and have had to come to terms early with physical limitation.

I have been asked how I could possibly write from the point of view of a heterosexual man. I grew up with a father and brother. I have worked with men in my professional life and have close male friends. I am, like them, attracted to women.

In the course of writing a dozen books, I have included all kinds of characters, male and female, gay and straight, American, Canadian, English, Japanese, black and white, one-armed, working class, upper-middle class, and they've had a wide variety of jobs and a great range of personal experiences. In each instance, if I am asked how I can write about being a black draft dodger or an electronic-music composer or a father, there are explanations within my own experience, connections and affinities.

Offering personal credentials, however, doesn't really explain why characters seem believable. A character has to have a magnetic core which attracts detail of all kinds, and out of that rich rubble comes the material by which a writer shapes and moves the character. Only some of those details can be traced. Many of them have been attracted from the subconscious or magpie consciousness of the writer.

Characters in fiction are not real people any more than photographs are real people. A believable or authentic character is a plausible composition made out of words. A writer doesn't have to become a character in the sense that an actor does, whose body is as important as the dialogue for creating the image. But even with the enormous limitation of her own body, a good actor can present a surprising range of characters, even, in the skin of one, age twenty years in an hour. We know it's not really happening, and perhaps the distinction between reality and art is clearer on the stage than in a novel. We know that asking an actor to play no one but herself would be denying her the basic point of her craft.

Deception is so much a part of acting that it is underlined to the delight of the audience. Gender deception, for instance, is the stuff of comedy. Long after boys were required to play women's parts on the Elizabethan stage, which invited ironic unmaskings of gender itself, actors have been challenged to play roles of the opposite sex. But rarely is deception the only point. There is something to be learned, a new insight to be gained.

Because in fiction a writer is usually invisible, it may be easier to confuse art with reality, to form suspicions about authenticity that have nothing to do with art.

By a willing suspension of disbelief, we allow ourselves to experience another's idea of reality. We must always be willing to risk that if we are to gain insight into who we are as individuals in our own culture. Misogynists are not necessarily telling lies about women when they express their genuine dislike. The same is true of racists and snobs. We'll not cure them of biases we don't approve of by silencing them, but we can help to cure the world of their power by expressing world views that are different from theirs. We must, however, claim the world as our own to do so, not be inhibited by any narrow view of what our authentic voices are. The first essay I ever wrote was the assignment, "I am part of all that I have met." I wrote for days and days. There was no end to it, nor should there be. It's an assignment I won't have completed even when I've written my last word.

Robertson Davies may write all he wants about lesbians as long as I may write all I want about men like Robertson Davies. We are both concerned, in our own ways, about gender disturbance. On the whole, I think it's a good thing. My characters, clothed in whatever gender, are deceptions in search of the truth.

# OUR MOTHERS

{ September 2005 }

Most of the great women writers of the past were childless. Not only obvious lesbians like Gertrude Stein and Radclyffe Hall and spinsters like Jane Austen and the Brontës but George Eliot, George Sand, Elizabeth Barrett Browning, and Virginia Woolf. All for various reasons avoided motherhood.

Since the 1950s a remarkable number of the best-known writers of Canada have been women and the great majority of them have also been mothers. Margaret Atwood, Marian Engel, Margaret Laurence, Alice Munro, Carol Shields and Audrey Thomas come quickly to mind.

All have had long productive careers. Aside from Margaret Atwood, who had her daughter after she had established herself

17

as a writer, the others were all contending with small children at the same time they were serving their apprenticeships as writers, Marian Engel with twins, Audrey Thomas and Alice Munro with three daughters each, Carol Shields with five children!

These post-World War II women did not grow up expecting to have it all, marriage, children, and a career. At most they probably expected to work at part-time jobs until their husbands were better established and the babies began to arrive. Writing was not a practical way of increasing the family income. In fact, it cost money to write. Someone else had to be paid to mind the children in day care or at home if a woman were to have any time alone at her desk or the kitchen table. Publishing a poem or a short story might boost the morale of a beginning writer but certainly not practically justify the investment of time. Writing was an expensive, self-indulgent habit, fostered guiltily in the very early morning, late at night, in snatches during the day as the children got older.

For those whose marriages survived such selfish, self-indulgent behavior, aids other writers depended on like Canada Council grants and part-time teaching were harder to come by. What does a married woman need with government support or a job when she has a husband to pay the bills? For those who found themselves single parents Canada Council might be more generous, but jobs were even harder to come by, for many bosses were unwilling to hire women whose sick children might get in the way of work.

I had been given two Canada Council grants before Margaret Laurence got her first. I was offered tenure in the Writing Department at the University of British Columbia where Audrey

Thomas had been refused a job because she had children. She was apparently supposed to stay home with them even if she couldn't feed them.

Against these odds, all these women did begin to publish, but they were reviewed less widely than their male counterparts, and the public readings and publicity tours which were being established were often out of reach for them because of their children. When they were reviewed or interviewed, they were often referred to not as writers but as "housewives" with a hobby. Or their femininity was called into question. Margaret Laurence's most disliked caption under her photograph was "mannish but motherly." Earlier in her career Margaret Atwood said she wouldn't be interviewed at home or asked personal questions because the first one would be, "When is Graeme leaving you?"

It was bad enough to scribble at home, a vice like secretly gorging on chocolate, but to publish was to confess openly that you routinely neglected your family for the vanity of public attention. For what most writers earned, no one could be accused of material greed.

Against charges of being castrators, child abusers, vain delusionaries, these women, these wives and mothers, along with dozens of others, have persisted while also carrying the burden of all artists in this country, where there is room at the top only for the few survivors. They have become among the most loved and appreciated writers not only in Canada but in the English speaking world, honored by awards, honorary degrees, Orders of Canada. Their work is taught in schools and universities. They are household names, inspirations to generations of women coming after them that, yes, it is possible to do it all. Not without a terrible price, some would say: a failed marriage, a drinking problem, a child burdened with a famous parent.

Success is costly and often not in ways that can be anticipated or easily paid for. But failure is too, and the world, so much the richer for its artists, is also poorer for those whose voices and visions were silenced by its bigoted inhospitality to their dreams.

In a time of cutbacks to services for women and children, for the arts, the difficulties faced by young mothers today who also want to write are enormous. But they do have, as generations before them didn't, literary mothers who have been mothers themselves and given us a literature richer for that experience. They have transcended or changed the meaning of "women's literature." Canada's voice in world literature is, as often as not, a woman's voice, a mother's voice, now being joined by the voices of women around the world.

# TEACHERS AND CRITICS

{ Undated }

The first thing I remember about learning to write is that I wasn't allowed to use my left hand. The first thing I remember about learning to read is "See Dick run." An early grammar lesson went, "If you say 'I ain't got no lunch' that means you have some lunch because two negatives make a positive."

There are so many punitive assumptions in our teaching of language that it's a daunting task to begin to uproot and examine them to see what values they actually support and what kinds of damage they have done and go on doing first in our schools before they find their judgmental way into the voices of our critics.

Unlike most other disciplines, such as math, science, and geography, language does not need to be taught, for a six-year-old child is already equipped with an understanding of its basic structures and is already in oral command of it. All that is left to be learned is to get it on and off paper, to make the sound of language visible. Vast numbers of people have lived and died without the skills of reading and writing. And though we pay lip service to the value of universal education, the rate of illiteracy in North America is embarrassingly high. A great many people who have learned to read and write grow up and grow old terrified of being tested in those skills because the learning of them was such a long exercise in humiliation.

I've often pondered how many people don't write their Members of Parliament or letters to the editor because they think they don't know how to spell. I know the young in my family dread writing to me because I've been that threatening creature, an English teacher, dedicated to getting it through their heads that the language they started out thinking of as their own to do with what they pleased really belongs to the cultural police, who are determined to keep it a white, élitist, masculine force, imposing those standards on everyone else.

I have enormous admiration for the courage of children who go on writing, and writing what they think and feel, against the bloodying of every attempt they make with that vicious weapon, the red pencil. But the large majority of us, by the time we are grown, have stopped trying.

I once used "I" in an essay in a high school English class, and the comment in the margin was, "Who do you think you are?" My simple, puzzled answer was, "the writer of this essay." Becoming visible in my writing seemed to me one way of taking responsibility for it, but I was being taught that the only way I might grow up to be a critic was to disappear into my own prose and pretend I was taking dictation from the voice of god. The god of language has a million proclamations, only a few having to do with meaning. The god of language says that if you don't got no lunch, you'll starve until you learn how to express your need properly. If we studied other languages more, or even the history of our own, we'd find out that god is really a cranky eighteenth-century grammarian who didn't like the double negative, used in so many other languages for emphasis, and used in English, too, until he came along at a time when people were getting more organized about education so that he had an opportunity to apply his single will to "reforming" the language. A hungry kid doesn't know that, but a teacher should.

There are, of course, good teachers who don't spend all their time setting up bad examples of grammar to be corrected, not because their meaning is unclear but because they are "improper" uses of the language. Instead they encourage their students to write as the only sure way to learn that skill, and, if spelling is corrected at all, the misspelled word is given back to the student correctly spelled for his or her own dictionary. The word becomes a gift from teacher to student rather than a wound on the page. A good teacher reads and hears, instructs by offering new skills as a student is ready to develop them. It's an approach as useful in university classes as it is in first grade. For against the great social negatives of language, which teach people that nearly no one has the right to use it, certainly not in public, there must be a strong and continuing struggle to show people that language really does belong to them and is for their use.

Critics who see their roles as basically judgmental, to bloody and humble anyone whose work does not please them, have joined the cultural police, there to be sure that those of the wrong grammatical persuasion are silenced. If they pretend they have no such power, let them consider Thomas Hardy, who gave up writing novels because he became so discouraged by the vitriolic attacks on his books. He also tried to please the critics by giving up regional words in his poems until, in his old age, he looked one up in the dictionary, found it there, and found himself quoted as the source. Even he didn't know the language belonged to him until he found evidence for it in a book. Kafka only survived as a writer by putting everything he wrote in a trunk.

The dismissive arrogance of the critic not only threatens to silence those who have dared to write but contributes to the climate which keeps many from ever making the attempt. There simply are a lot of people who can't stand the heat in the kitchen but are, nevertheless, very good cooks.

There are good critics, too. How else did *The Color Purple* win the National Book Award? I did hear someone say, "Well, they knew Alice Walker could write proper English when she wanted to."

A good critic must first be a generous reader, in search of value to be shared with readers. Honest reservations have to be examined first for hidden prejudices before they are included in any comment. In my experience, the few critics with a real capacity to judge a work's value are rarely much interested in that aspect of the job, far more interested in using their superior knowledge to give readers greater access to the work at hand. If it really isn't worth their attention, they don't write about it. At those rare times when a book seems important enough to denounce, it should be a matter of great grief rather than a crowing triumph.

Critics, like teachers, should be showing us how to be better, more generous readers, as well as confident and hard-working writers. Without good critics we are in real danger of losing our voices, the birthright of our language, to those convinced we have no such right.

# DREAMING

{ 2005 }

I have always had to struggle against boredom
with other people's dreams, whether at the breakfast table or
in books, and only intermittently put much store in my own,
unable to put faith in Freudian sexual codes or Jungian theories
of a collective unconscious. The climate of dreams seems to me
like the climate of the world, unpredictable. I feel as sympathetic
with the weatherman as I do with psychologists and palm and
tea leaf readers from whom we ask impossible insights into our
natures and futures.

I have saved and used only one dream from my childhood,
the year I started school in California in 1936, the middle of
the Depression, among children of various races and class

backgrounds. In my class the two most popular boys, Wally, Chinese, and Chioki, Japanese, were nearly always chosen as captains of opposing teams at recess, our childish reflection of the war then going on between China and Japan. One night I had a Gulliver dream of being tied down in my bed by Japanese soldiers, the size my brother and I made with lead molds for waging wars in the backyard. These tiny soldiers marched across the headboard of my bed and down across my body, spinning like spiders a network of ropes until I was immobilized. The next evening, sitting on my father's lap between him and his newspaper, I asked, "How big are Jap soldiers?" "Small," he replied, "very small." It hasn't been for me an insight into my own five-year-old psyche so much as a reminder of how young children are when the world's troubles rile their dreams, how little the most well-meaning adults can help.

I don't mean to suggest that dreams are useless. I have often had the experience of going to sleep with a problem, more often about the fiction I was writing than about my personal life, and awakened to find it solved without any recollection of a dream. The unconscious functioning of the brain doesn't seem to need either recall or analysis to do its work. I even suspect such conscious interference can limit or damage the process. In the forty-some-odd years when writing was my chief occupation, I noticed, if I hadn't been writing for a while, I began to dream without images, nothing but streams of sentences in a void. It was a signal to me that I must get back to work for my psychic health, a simple "use it or lose it" message for the imagination.

Dreams, recalled or not, can affect the emotional climate of the day, make me more amiable or apprehensive, but it hasn't seemed to me particularly helpful to try to retrieve the sources of that pleasure or anxiety. Rather the task is to harness their power for the tasks of the day. Nor have I brooded much on the morality of the unconscious, tried instead to be stoic in enduring the punishments inflicted by overindulgence, a bad conscience, fear, as I also accept erotic, comic, and cosmic wonders without wondering much why I deserve them, if I do.

To search for meaning in a dream, as if that dream were a code to be cracked, an insight or message inherent in it, is to me like looking for a jar of jam in a blackberry patch, a loaf of bread in a field of wheat. Meaning is not found; it is made from whatever lies within and about us. We don't search for and then find love or a world to live in. We either make them or do without. Dreams are only one of the many raw materials which may work overnight like yeast in bread dough, ready in the morning for the heat of patience, will, intelligence and imagination that can truly feed our hunger for what matters.

# LABELS

{ March 2005 }

From the time we are very young children we are taught to label ourselves and other people in a variety of ways. But what begins as simple information soon becomes more complicated, colored by value judgments which are not always fixed or easy to understand. I was five before I learned that being a girl had serious drawbacks, six before I discovered that being left-handed was unacceptable, nineteen and traveling in Europe for the first time before I had to apologize for being an American. Some labels we can choose like a favorite hat; some we are simply stuck with like a necessary cane. Those we outgrow like "child" are replaced by "old woman." Others we are comfortable with only after they really apply, as I am now with the label "writer."

By the time I was fifteen, I was sure I wanted to be a writer and I wasn't shy of saying so. What kind of a writer I wasn't yet sure. I was writing a lot of bad poetry, strongly metered and rhymed in imitation of Edna St Vincent Millay and Elinor Wylie, inspired for subject matter even by such heavy worthies as Milton. When my mother read my tragically touching, thumpingly rhymed poem on my own blindness, she laughed and saved the world from the bad poet I might have grown up to be. I retreated for a time to personal essays intended to amuse, and my mother, for whom laughter was the highest goal, approved. When I reached college at sixteen, away from my mother's comic influence, I began to write bad short stories in imitation of Katherine Anne Porter and Eudora Welty, heavy in symbolism and grotesque characters. One featured a black man with yellow hair and green eyes, named Cain, who raped sheep. That story inspired my classmates to burst into the Wiffenpoof song—"We are little black sheep who have gone astray, bah, bah, bah"—every time they saw me.

Tough critics like my mother and my classmates daunted me a little. Then I learned that in academic circles a real writer was by definition dead. Those foolish enough to be alive were not real writers at all, but "creative" writers, a swell-headed, deluded lot with nothing important to say. That attitude taught me, if not real modesty, some caution about exposing my ambitions. I gradually learned not to call myself a writer at all. As a young university teacher, I did not admit that what I did in my spare time was write short stories and novels. During the ten years I wrote before I had any publishing success, writing was a secret vice to be confessed only to intimate friends.

A few years ago the Writers' Union of Canada was concerned about how few young writers were applying for membership and tried to think of ways to make them more welcome. I pointed out that it was, in fact, very difficult to admit to being a writer. Only years of experience which tended to thicken the skin made such a confession possible. In my personal world I came out as a lesbian long before I came out as a writer. The Union should be resigned to being an organization for the middle-aged and the old.

I finished my third novel, which would be my first to be published, a few days before my thirtieth birthday. It took three years to find publishers. I don't know what I expected beyond finally feeling I might have a legitimate claim to call myself a writer, or, if not anything as grand on the slim proof of one published book (anyone can write one book), at least be permitted to say that I wrote. Instead, in 1964, before homosexual relationships were removed from the criminal code, I became Canada's only visible lesbian and almost lost my job at the University of British Columbia. I was defended by my colleagues with the old saw, "Writers of murder mysteries are not necessarily murderers." To my interviewers I was not a writer but a sexual deviant.

Years later my good friend Don Bailey told me that, in all his years of publishing poems and stories and novels, no interviewer ever wanted him to talk about his writing, which he began in jail serving a term as a bank robber. They wanted him to talk about robbing banks. Over a bottle of Scotch, we decided we should have a TV program called "The Lesbian and the Bank Robber" and give the public what they apparently want.

José Saramago, in his novel *Blindness*, says that if we first contemplated all the possible ramifications of our words or actions, we would be struck dumb and freeze. We can't possibly know and therefore take responsibility for the effect our words may have on others. As Auden says in "In Memory of W.B. Yeats," poetry is "modified in the guts of the living." Certainly Goethe, when he wrote *The Sorrows of Young Werther*, didn't intend or expect to inspire a rash of suicides all across Europe. Yet we are often expected, like parents, to take responsibility for what our work, however distorted and misrepresented, does out in the world.

I am also labeled a pornographer because my books, coming from the States where some stay longer in print than they have in Canada, are routinely seized at the border by Customs, but none has finally ever been refused entry. Still the label sticks, and readers who buy my books are therefore often disappointed, and others who might otherwise buy and enjoy them don't.

I have done relatively little to publicize my work, weary of the roles I've been forced to play, but, when I agree to be interviewed, I give up any notion of speaking as a writer and become instead a teacher about gay issues, about censorship, about civil liberties, a responsibility I take seriously, not so much as a writer but as a citizen.

My first published novel came out just before I became a Canadian citizen. It is a book set in the States, probably accurately called an American novel. I have since been challenged about what right I have to call myself a Canadian writer, though the majority of my fiction has been set in Canada. My Dutch publisher, arranging a publication party for one of my novels, approached the Canadian Embassy for a small contribution, only to be told that I was really an American. "Odd," replied my publisher, "since another branch of your government contributed funds for translating the book." I have been told that some Canadian writers traveling abroad are pleased to be mistaken for American and therefore part of a larger and more established and respected tradition. Only strong nationalists like Margaret Atwood insist on being identified as Canadian and become ambassadors for Canadian literature. For immigrants (another possible label) it is often difficult to know what use there is or what right we have to claim our citizenship as part of our identity. I felt guilty the first time I traveled in Europe with a Canadian passport and enjoyed the courtesy and kindness so often withheld from Americans, for underneath that bland label lurked surely still an ugly American. I should probably have been called an ex-American writer. Even now, after fifty years in this country and very proud and relieved to be a Canadian, I am shy to claim the label and never surprised if others are reluctant to grant it.

With Margaret Atwood: "ambassadors for Canadian literature."

Because only a very few fiction writers or poets make even a modest living from those activities, many turn to other forms of writing to pay the rent. Betty Jane Wylie, a playwright and poet, as well as a wife and mother of four children, was widowed suddenly in her forties and faced the task of not only raising four children alone but supporting them as well. She was amazingly successful, writing books of advice for widows, cookbooks, writers' guidebooks, travel books, while she also occasionally took time to write a poem or play. Recently she was awarded the Order of Canada. An interviewer, seeing listed among her many accomplishments a book on using leftovers, wanted her advice on how to use up what was in his refrigerator. She snapped back "I don't suppose I was given the Order of Canada because I know how to clean out your fridge." Genre labels make most writers uncomfortable in a culture that rates writing narrowly and strictly to exclude, or at least place below the salt, how-to books or children's books or mysteries or science fiction as not really literature. Even best-sellers and women's fiction are suspect. A poet isn't a real poet if he or she is funny or sings poems to a guitar accompaniment. Genre labels are not meant to be descriptive so much as judgmental. Real writers don't write cookbooks or jokes or murder mysteries. Real writers die of starvation years before they can reap the rewards of their immortal words. And their names are often "Anon."

Though some claim that "Anon" was a woman, gender labeling of writers has been a long debate. Many women writers in the past chose to avoid the label with masculine pen names, and that still is the habit of some mystery and science fiction writers who fear otherwise putting off their male readers. One bookseller

I know makes a habit of misleading men into buying women's writing so disguised. Until the present women's movement made many women rethink their attitudes toward themselves as women, even writers who didn't disguise their gender often refused to be included in women's anthologies or published in women's magazines, not wanting to be ghettoized.

Certainly some gay writers resist the label, not now so much in fear of criminal charges or job loss or alienation from family but of being placed in an even smaller ghetto, cut off from the mainstream of literature, from larger audiences of readers.

Disguised or denied sexual identity rarely works. The first novel of James Baldwin's I read was *Giovanni's Room*, a story of two white male homosexuals in France. I didn't know Baldwin was black until I read others of his books, less self-conscious and much more powerful when he wasn't hiding his race or his sexuality in white characters. Who we really are nourishes what we write, and energy is better spent transcending than denying limiting labels. That choice also has the virtue of inspiring great loyalty in core audiences, ethnic, racial, sexual, who will be there for us even if the cross-over audiences publishers are always wooing don't happen to cross.

If we could be identified as many-labeled, which all of us are, we might move more comfortably in the world. Even if we could wear only those labels appropriate for the occasion, much as we select among our shirts or rings, we would be less apt to be embarrassed and irritable.

Auden said, "I am a poet only when I'm writing a poem." Because writers so often feel they may possibly never write another worthwhile word, putting down the label except while involved in the activity can be an enormous relief. For a long time I wanted to be even freer than that. I didn't want to be a writer at all. I simply wanted to write and being a writer got in the way of that, because what the world wants of a writer is not writing but public performing, lectures, readings, seminars, for which we are often paid more than we are for the writing we do. Now that I am retired, write only very occasionally as with this small essay, which seems like a grandchild come to visit for a few days, I don't find it as difficult to "be a writer." But the old are forgetful of nouns. Proper nouns go first, then common nouns. They are, after all, the only words we have to teach children who learn other parts of speech, even verbs and their tenses, by themselves. We are not finally labelers. The real business of our lives is to live, to love, to write, and to remember, leaving the calling of names to others, names we may answer to or not.

# CENSORSHIP

{ Undated }

Censorship begins with what D.H. Lawrence called "the voices of our education." The Christian preschool I attended opened each morning with chapel, at the end of which we were allowed to ask any questions we had. I asked why God was better than Santa Claus when Santa Claus brought presents. I was put in the closet where the hockey sticks were stored. When my grandmother and great-aunt were arguing about the pattern to choose for a place setting of silver for my Uncle Harry, I asked, "What difference does it make since he's blind?" I was sent to my room for twenty-four hours. My mother tried to explain to me what I wasn't supposed to say. I shouldn't make remarks about how people looked. (I'd just asked a man why his teeth were so long.) It was better not to talk about religion. She wasn't sure it had been a good idea for me to name one of my dolls Jesus Christ because it prompted me to make such observations as "I left Jesus out in the rain last night" or "There's Jesus under the couch." I did try. I hadn't really any wish to offend people. One day I looked at my mother and said, "Gosh, you're getting fat," and then thought, oh, I'm sure that's one of those things I'm not supposed to say, but she only responded mildly with, "Am I, dear?" My younger sister was born a couple of months later.

The first voice of my education in print was "See Dick run." Right through "The Landing of the Pilgrim Fathers" to *David Copperfield* and on into college with Shakespeare and Milton, that command persisted. Women and minorities in literature are invisible or subservient as they are supposed to be in life. This Jane never learned to be as good as the Jane in the reader at watching Dick run.

I didn't know, until long after I'd finished my formal education, that I'd been suffering from sexism. I went to a women's college and was taught by good women teachers. I was encouraged to go on into graduate school. Still I knew something was skewed, something didn't fit my kind of brain. The questions I posed about what I was reading were still inappropriate. Though I took American literature, I didn't discover Gertrude Stein or Willa Cather until later. The voices of my foremothers were not included in my education.

The publication of my first novel, *Desert of the Heart*, was delayed a year on legal advice to my publisher. The libel report was nearly as long as the book. Since I had invented the characters, I had no fear of being sued by any of them, but I had to make revisions as if my characters were recognizable people who could sue. I had to take the date out of the book (in a later edition I restored it), disguise the location, and my final task was to look up all my characters in the Reno telephone directory. I actually found one of them and had to change her name then and there so that I could check my new choice. These are not the ordinary exercises of an author preparing a book for publication. In the early '60s, novels were not being published about erotic relationships between women.

The climate had so changed in the '70s that I was commissioned by Doubleday to write *Lesbian Images*. When I decided to include a chapter on Willa Cather, my editor told me the Willa Cather Foundation would not allow me to quote from her works in such a book. I should leave her out of my study. I persisted and the Foundation, though it had persuaded other scholars to drop references to her lesbian experience, did give me the permissions I needed.

There was a mail strike in Canada when I was ready to send the manuscript to New York. A friend working near the border offered to take it across and mail it from Blaine. He was stopped, asked to open the parcel, then harassed by American Customs officials about taking dirty books across the border. When they finally let him through, they informed him that the post office in Blaine had shut for the day five minutes before.

I doubt that you'll find *Lesbian Images* in high school libraries, yet several young readers have written to me to say the book saved them from suicide.

Any book that doesn't "see Dick run" is subjected to the pervasive censorships of this culture, the biases of schools, editors, foundations, customs officials, before it is ever tested by our actual censorship laws.

The function of the voices of our education is to teach us to censor ourselves, and most of us do. We are social creatures, after all. We'd as soon not offend. But the values of this culture are becoming increasingly offensive to large numbers of its citizens. Racism, sexism and religious bigotry, all rampant in our literature and our dirty jokes alike, are beginning to be challenged.

Unfortunately the challenge sometimes comes in the form of requesting more rather than less censorship. It has not worked against pornography. It does more harm than good focused on hate literature. It has never protected us effectively from anything but some parts of the truth of experience. It's a cheap political weapon in the hands of a government willing to censor pictures of battered women but unwilling to spend money on shelters for the women themselves.

Prime Minister Brian Mulroney expressed surprise when he heard that Canada Customs was able to stop Salman Rushdie's *Satanic Verses* from coming into the country. He certainly didn't think Customs officials should have the power to decide what Canadians do and do not read. Yet Canada Customs has been routinely stopping shipments of books to gay bookstores for years, often withholding books that are freely shipped to other bookstores in Canada. Mulroney's surprise suggests that politicians don't really know the laws of Canada.

Politicians are not alone in their ignorance. Most people seem unaware of the routine use of censorship laws to persecute gay bookstores and gay publications. Thousands and thousands of tax payers' dollars have been spent to harass that community.

Our freedom to write and our freedom to read should be in no one's hands but our own. We must stand firm not only against more restrictive legislation but against the laws already on the books. But as important is our refusal to censor ourselves. If we don't, the voices of our education will go on teaching us and our children that only Dick has the right to run.

With brother Art. "This Jane never learned to be as good as the Jane in the reader."

# CANADIAN CUSTOMS

{ Undated }

The censoring of women's voices goes on in Canada in much the same way it does in other countries. We are underrepresented as published authors. Fewer of us in print are reviewed. The special agencies we set up, women's presses and women's bookstores, tend to reinforce our marginalization. Efforts are being made by the Writers' Union of Canada to educate and change the policy makers' attitudes toward women writers so that we are more equally represented not only in publishing and in review coverage but also on reading lists in all our educational institutions, but it is a battle fought alongside what is perceived as an even more urgent issue, which is seeing that Canadian writers are represented in our own schools and universities as well as in bookstores and on bookracks across the country. Only a very small percentage of the books sold in Canada are written by Canadians. No Canadian writer can make a living without reaching the wider audiences for French or English, our two official languages.

My experience of censorship as a Canadian woman writer is further colored by the fact that I am a lesbian. In my fiction I integrate lesbian and gay characters with a whole range of other people, a practice I have been told is more threatening to a heterosexual reader than containing lesbian and gay characters in their own subcultures.

In the 1960s, the Canadian audience for Canadian novels was so small that publishers had to find either an American or British publisher for a joint venture. In 1962 my first novel, *Desert of the Heart*, was therefore accepted by Secker and Warburg in England before a Canadian publisher could produce the book. Because the book dealt with lesbian lovers, in England it was subjected to an investigation for possible libel. No reassurance from me that all the characters were truly fictional satisfied the publisher, who insisted on my disguising settings, taking the date out of the book, even checking characters' names in appropriate telephone books. This exercise delayed publication for a year, but the book was reviewed widely both in Canada and England and is still in print in a number of languages today.

Though mainstream publishers have since become more accustomed to handling both feminist and gay subjects, their marketing skills for such books are limited since they depend on reviews and quick sales. Feminist and gay presses are willing to keep books in print long enough for them to sell by word of mouth, as they must because books from such presses are rarely reviewed. Only in Canada do I still publish with a mainstream press. In the States I publish with Naiad, a lesbian press. In England Pandora has reissued all my novels. In both countries there is critical silence about my work, and I am reviewed only in the gay and feminist media.

Canada is not as homophobic as either England or the States. My books are generally reviewed here, and I am invited to participate in the literary life of this country, which includes serving on juries for the Canada Council, our arts granting organization, and being sent abroad to represent Canada.

But at the borders of my own country, my books are subject to special customs surveillance if they are being sent to gay bookstores in Canada. Many of my books are out of print in Canada and must come into the country from England or the States. It is the policy of Canada Customs, as it has been of British Customs, routinely to detain books sent to gay bookstores. Though no book of mine has ever finally been banned in either country, some have been damaged or lost on their way to gay bookstores. Only a few months ago a novel of mine, *The Young in One Another's Arms*, which won the Canadian Authors' Association best novel of the year award in 1978, was detained at the Canadian border. The Writers' Union of Canada and the Civil Liberties Association are charging the government with contravening our Charter of Rights by allowing our customs officials the right to censor our reading.

Unlike England, where hostility to homosexuality is both sanctioned and encouraged by the government, Canada's recent concern is for greater legal protection for the rights of all minorities and for women. At least the ingrained prejudices are being acknowledged as prejudices rather than enshrined as cultural values. But our education as a citizenry open to the voices of women and particularly lesbians, women of color, and other minorities within our sex is far from complete.

Even if our Canadian house can be put in order, I, like all Canadian writers, depend also on audiences outside these borders. As long as the large chain bookstores in the States won't carry Naiad books, as long as Pandora Press in England receives less than its fair share of reviewing space, my books will continue to reach only a fraction of their real audience. And the voices of protest against the silencing of women and minorities are not as strong and well-organized in England and the States as they are here. Nor do those governments feel required, as ours does, to pay at least lip service to equal rights for women and minorities. In a country where we import the large majority of the books we read, even books written by our own writers, I am as much at the mercy of homophobia in England and the States as I am of the homophobia of Canadian customs officials. At least in Canada I can join the protests, but at the important sources of my publication I have no voice. The publishing centers of the English-speaking world silence more than their own citizens in a climate of imperial bigotry.

# THE VOICE OF WOMAN

{ Undated }

Browsing through a directory of the Writers' Union of Canada to get some of the bare bones of experience out of which Canadian women write, I was impressed by the number of women who have children. Though mothers are not unknown among women writers of the past, many of the most famous were either single or childless: Jane Austen, George Eliot, the Brontës, Gertrude Stein, Edith Sitwell, Virginia Woolf, Willa Cather, Amy Lowell, Emily Dickinson, Marianne Moore, Katherine Anne Porter, Eudora Welty, Carson McCullers, Flannery O'Connor, Ethel Wilson. Not all of them chose to be either single or childless, both options much more freely taken now when marriage is not so mercenary a business and birth control far more easily practiced. But being childless played a role in their freedom to write, in the size of their accomplishments.

I know, because I filled out the directory's forms myself, that we were asked to list mates and children. I'm interested to see that not everyone does. Margaret Atwood, Joan Haggerty and Gladys Hindmarch make no mention of mates or children, though I know they have had both. Daphne Marlatt doesn't give that information either, but she is pictured with her son. One woman makes only the claim of being a grandmother. No lesbian among us lists a mate and, since several of us have also been wives, mothers and even grandmothers, we are a very much buried statistic. Some of the men also refuse personal information, but they are bolder, when they feel like it, to list wife no.1 and children, wife no.2 and children or not.

Because I know a fair number of women in the directory, I understand why some of them choose to be silent about their personal lives, either because they are not so easily categorically described or because they are matters of regret, why some of them, like Christie Harris, proudly name husband and five children, and *look*, all those books as well. But her first book was published twenty-five years after her marriage. Margaret Atwood's first and only child, on the other hand, was born after ten books were in print.

A large majority of these women wanted children and are glad they have them, though very few would deny that being a mother robbed them of years of their writing lives. With life expectancy what it is now, a delayed career doesn't have to be a denied career. And, increasingly, younger women are postponing motherhood until they are established enough to afford the help they need to go on with their work.

What fewer of them are certain of is their roles as wives to first husbands, as the number of divorces, listed and unlisted, indicates. The voice of woman in Canadian letters is increasingly the voice of a divorced mother, and, as Audrey Thomas said recently in an interview, "There are a lot of those out there."

They know at very close quarters how little welcome there is for woman as equal partner, never mind as equal citizen. They write about a world that would silence them if it could. The women they create are victims or subversives or survivors. Margaret Atwood writes, "Marriage is not/ a house or even a tent/ it is before that, and colder." To warm herself Stacey, in Margaret Laurence's *The Fire-Dwellers*, drinks, takes an unlikely lover. Margaret Atwood writes, "You take my hand and/ I'm suddenly in a bad movie," which might be from Audrey Thomas's *Latakia*, in which Rachel tries to be part of a triangle with her lover Michael and his wife Hester, and fails. Joan, in Atwood's *Lady Oracle*, writes gothic romances to escape for a while her Polish Count and then Arthur, and finally plans to vanish altogether in her own fictional death. There are moments of bitterness, rage, despair in these books, but all of them are finally about surviving not villainous men but the institution that has trapped men and women together with different needs and expectations, with unequal powers.

Yet beyond that institution lies the territory of single parenthood, where making a living is even harder. Harriet, in Engel's *Lunatic Villas*, is tending a houseful of children, only one of whom is hers, all deserted in one way or another. She supports them by writing a column called "Depressed Housewife," on subjects like abortion, welfare wives, and children of divorce. "I've never been one of the admired and don't expect to be, but I'm one of the competent," Harriet says, and so she is, in her own terms and free to set them. But the domestic chaos she lives in might not inspire a reader to emulate her choices. This is the only novel by these women in which a man is entirely loving and sympathetic, but unfortunately he died before the opening of the story.

Stacey's husband is no monster, neither is Michael in *Latakia*, nor are the Polish Count and Arthur in *Lady Oracle*. They are simply human-size, which is hard on men who expect to be seen as heroes, at least in the eyes of their wives and children. That women writers are often sympathetic to that need doesn't push them into lying to fulfill it. When men ask women for "understanding," what they mean is sympathy and forgiveness, not insight into their real motives. Women's writing is full of real motives. More than once a woman has sighed, "If only men really were superior, it would be a possible world." Since they are not, the only realistic choices are to make an equal partnership or go on alone. But it takes living the lie for a time, sometimes even a lifetime, to know that.

How often I laugh aloud when I'm reading Marian Engel or Margaret Atwood or Audrey Thomas or Margaret Laurence, not because they are working for laughs but because laughter bubbles up, life-affirming, in the mess and miracle of female living. They show women in their nurturing roles, tending, offering sympathy, sacrificing themselves, but their women are also more perceptive, critical and even defiant than women are supposed to be, if not for themselves, then for their children.

The domestic novel has never held a high place with contemporary critics, whether in Jane Austen's time or our own. As Austen mocked her own craft, so the women characters who write in these Canadian novels write "trash," the time-wasters of wives and mothers who should be getting on with their real work. At the domestic novel's best—and we have superlatively good writers of them in this country—it offers women sometimes the only honest company they can find for sources of insight, self-respect, laughter, and courage.

More men are reading domestic novels, too, finding in them women who are neither whores nor saints, men who are neither villains nor heroes but very much like themselves, in need of the real insights they find about ambition, vanity, and the power to rationalize, about a laughter they can learn to share.

The voices only beginning to be heard are from those women who have chosen other women as partners, either early or later in life, with the hope of a better kind of relationship. Many of us are divorced mothers, too. The difficulties of women living together may teach us that the problems between people cannot be reduced to differences in gender, that what keeps women in their place is not simply the greater power of men but women's own concepts of what it is to be a woman. But also such experience may show how much is really up for negotiation, how great the variety of choices really is, whether between men and women or between women.

# THE PUBLIC GOOD

{ February 2004 }

F̶ree speech and literature would not need to
be defended against censorship if we never were offended by
what other people say or write. Dissent is a basic freedom in a
democracy because it is an individual's chief defense against
those in power who might otherwise abuse that power to invade
our privacy, restrict our right to know, dictate our beliefs. That
we are sometimes exposed to ideas that are hateful, degrading
or just plain stupid is the price we must be willing to pay for a
freedom so essential to our public health.

Censorship of pornography in Canada, as in the new bill
against child pornography, has been both a cheap and cynical
device of the government to placate citizens concerned with the

vulnerability of women and children to those who abuse them. It costs the state little to attack images of abuse while millions of dollars are being diverted from programs that address the facts of abuse. Low welfare rates and minimum wages, plus a lack of affordable housing, women's shelters, rape relief centers and child care, have increased the poverty and vulnerability of women and children across the country. The government is the chief and most dangerous abuser.

We don't need laws against pornography which are more often used to intimidate and silence sexual minorities (witness the years in court of *The Body Politic* and Little Sister's bookstore) than to curb hard-core heterosexuality. It took irate citizens' fire-bombing of Vancouver video porn shops before the police pressed charges, which resulted in small fines and business as usual the next day. If actual children are being used in pornographic films, the images are evidence for criminal prosecution of the abusers. There is no more point in censoring acts of the imagination in art or literature than there would be in charging writers of murder mysteries or scriptwriters of mass butcheries like *The Lord of the Rings*. It is not through censorship of images that we can be taught whom and what we are not allowed to hate, whom and what we are not allowed to desire. Knowledge, not lack of it, is our best defense against the darkest of our desires, even when they are masked in morality and artistic merit as in Dante's *Inferno* or Shakespeare's *The Taming of the Shrew*.

The new child pornography law excludes the defense of artistic merit but allows an argument for public good. Moral justification, "the public good" is a concept that for years meant no homosexual relationship could be portrayed unless it was exposed as sick or depraved, the protagonists reformed or punished. The Hollywood happy ending for lesbians was typically marriage for one, suicide for the other. Presumably, under the new law, children could still be depicted as abused as long as the abuser is finally castrated or killed, no matter in what bad taste.

Censorship is a bad teacher, a government cop-out, and a danger to the basic freedoms on which democracy depends, on which the public good depends.

# CHOOSING HOME

{ 1997 }

I was still a child when I gave up trying to make myself at home. Someone always then put me in my place instead. To be born is to invade other people's territory, and by the time a child is ambulatory, it is alien to domestic order, cribbed and playpenned, sometimes even tied out of harm's way. To earn even marginal freedom is to learn to hear the hiss of danger everywhere from the butts in the ashtray to the cord on the lamp, from the potatoes in the bin to the wishbones drying on the chandelier. There is nothing cozy or comfy or safe no matter how many grown-up laps, cups of cocoa, and lullabies try to offer that illusion.

I first lived in a mock-Norman castle built by my grandfather to advertise a housing development. The room I shared with my older brother had a balcony which overlooked the living room and from which we could spy on the adult world. When I was three, we moved to an ordinary house where I had a room of my own, which meant no more to me than that I had to stay out of my brother's unless invited in. Mine was a place where I was sent until I could behave. At school I ended up in the hockey stick closet for the same reason. I was slow to learn the rules, then puzzled by them or forgetful of them.

"Your child will be run over by a car while you're explaining why she should get out of the street," my grandmother complained.

We were only under grandparental scrutiny intermittently. We moved again and again, outrunning the Depression, then at the edge of war. Sometimes we lived in other people's furnished houses while we waited for our own belongings to arrive, held up by a dock strike, a lost shipment. We learned to move as lightly as ghosts in places where other people's clothes hung in the closets, other children's toys were out of bounds on the screen porch. Released into a house in which we were expected to settle, we were less enthusiastic than our parents about stocking shelves with familiar objects, hanging pictures, unrolling rugs. If there was a room away, in the attic or basement or out over the garage, my brother was given it. I envied him that independence, but I wonder now if he didn't each time have some sense of banishment. My room was usually larger than my younger sister's because I had to have twin beds and share with any guest, usually a grandmother who draped underpants over the bedside lamp and ate sticky candied fruit into the night.

My transient suburban childhood was not an unusual experience at that time when Depression and then war dislodged a great many people, but it was not yet an accepted or expected way of life. Our grandparents lived in houses in which their children had grown up, even in houses where they had grown up themselves, attics and basements full of the accumulation of generations, the sorts of things we sold at yard sales every time we moved. When we went "home," it was to another generation's childhood where we were expected to have the manners and skills of country children. Of a summer we nearly learned to milk a cow, pluck a chicken, shoot a rabbit, quilt, embroider, preserve, but those lessons atrophied over the long suburban winters, during which we needed to learn how high to wear our socks, how to comb our hair, what sort of lunch box to carry. What was visible was relatively easy. Attitudes were harder to come by, whom to admire, whom to ignore. A form of respect in one community ("Yes, sir." "No, ma'am.") was not acceptable in another, ("Yes, Mrs Bolton." "No, Mr Dively."). Most of the kids we met had had only one telephone number and one address through their whole lives; what they thought and how they behaved was what everyone thought and how everyone behaved. They were at home. We were not. In New Jersey, California, Illinois, Missouri, and Kentucky we were never at home.

I would not have said I had a geographic identity until I took my first trip to Europe. It was soon after the war. I was nineteen. For the first time in my life I was not simply an outsider. I was an American about whom there were all sorts of negative expectations, a number of which I inadvertently fulfilled: jumping queues, speaking aloud in train compartments, being unnecessarily generous with cigarettes, expecting friendliness. But gradually my hard-earned adaptive skills brought me that grand compliment, "You don't seem like an American at all." At the end of that summer I phoned my parents from New York to tell them I'd had a safe crossing. "Gosh," I said to my mother, "you sound American." "I am American!" came the indignant reply.

I had pledged allegiance to the flag of the United States of America in dozens of classrooms all across the country, but the "justice and liberty for all" part of it had translated years ago into "bias and custom," "bigotry and conformity." And now I watched those distortions being acted out on the national stage with Joe McCarthy and his hearings, the new loyalty oath demanded of people in government and universities.

In 1956 I joined the migration north, a latter-day Empire loyalist, a precursor of Vietnam draft dodgers, and found in Vancouver a population of foreigners, immigrants from all over the world in a city whose downtown was still mainly parking lots. The sea and the abrupt mountains on the north shore provided the setting for a city yet to be built.

I moved into furnished digs, chosen for a fine, old roll-top desk and a grand view of the mountains, in which I intended to continue my apprenticeship as a writer. Like everywhere else I had lived, it was more a stage set than a home, with no more than a few familiar belongings. If I hadn't then begun to share my life with a woman with experience and need of home, I might never have graduated into an apartment we had to furnish ourselves. Among her other household goods, Helen brought with her a family dining room table, marked at the edges by a teething sister. The chairs included two with arms, my first experience of the comfort and power of heading our own table. But the apartment itself was confining without view or garden, and Helen was soon walking the neighborhood in search of a house to buy.

All my life I'd bought things with a mind to how well they would pack or store. I checked a shirt to be wrinkle-free before I tried it on, bought books but never paintings which would have to be crated for a move. I had borrowed furniture or made do with what could be left behind. Owning a house was a fantasy of stability beyond my imagining, and it frightened me. Only the reluctance of the mortgage broker to grant a mortgage to two women without the signature of a man restored my courage. What I discovered about owning a house was that it was a place where things could be left behind in their own places and returned to again and again. A trip to Europe no longer meant an uprooting. Home was a place you could leave behind intact, and it would be there for you when you got back.

I was in my early thirties before I really learned to make myself at home. We had found only a few blocks from where we lived a large, old house with a big garden and marvelous views of the sea, city and mountains. It had been lived in by a family with five children, the upstairs a rabbit warren of small bedrooms which we transformed into one grand bedroom and bath and Helen's study. The master bedroom on the ground floor became my study. In the high basement we put in rooms for students in winter, for guests in summer, a workshop for an old printing press and wine-making equipment. There I learned the names of trees, shrubs and flowers in the old garden and helped to re-design it as our own.

"George," Jane and Helen's Vancouver home.

In the twenty years we lived in one neighborhood, I learned not only the names but needs of our neighbors. I knew whose dog barked, whose kid practiced the trumpet. I knew the names of the clerks in the local stores, a baker who could make us an emergency wedding cake for a friend, a butcher who could help us impress guests with a crown roast.

Being at home expanded from the neighborhood into the city, where we helped to establish the Arts Club, meeting many of the writers, painters, actors, musicians, and architects who were involved in shaping the cultural life of Vancouver, building its much needed theatres, galleries and museums. We wrote letters of protest against the design of the new post office, forced the *Vancouver Sun* to keep and then expand its book page to include reviews of Canadian books, aired our views on local radio stations, went to each other's performances and openings, and imported artists from elsewhere.

Jane and Helen's home on Galiano Island.

Then I was asked to attend the founding meeting of the Writers' Union of Canada. Over those years I had become not only a writer but a Canadian writer with national responsibilities to my tribe and my culture, even eventually a representative of Canada abroad.

The first time I traveled with a Canadian passport, I had some sense of guilt in accepting kindness and welcome at every hand. Surely I hadn't changed so much as to be unrecognizable as the ugly American traveler I had once been. Gradually I learned simply to be grateful that the citizenship I'd chosen packs and travels so well.

Writing for me has always been a means of making sense of experience. The rootless richness of my childhood gave me lots of options and few assumptions; perhaps it took me longer to discover what has been mine to say and how to welcome my readers into the worlds I make, but the compensation has been that I was free to choose what home is, what I have needed it to be.

# NEITHER CURSE NOR BLESSING

{ March 1995 }

Being struck by lightning is as unlikely as winning the lottery. Yet some of us live in dread, in hope, unable by temperament to avoid anticipation of those drastic changes in fortune that accidental death or riches would bring. We feel as destined to the unlikely as characters in fiction or drama who fall heir to unexpected wealth or suffer dramatic deaths. Plot, that moral god of literature which rewards and punishes so grandly, must, we plead, invade our lives as well so that we are not forever left in the audience, grieving and envying the fates of those chosen to have them. We are not, however, all "actors upon the stage;" we are in the pit or gallery, satisfying our appetite for fate vicariously on a diet of the erotic and melodramatic, aroused and terrified, in search of a catharsis that has little or nothing to do with our own lives.

Art misleads us. To be murdered or crowned are not defining moments. They are simply the metaphors for our fears and longings. Does anyone, in fact, want to fly high enough to fall out of the sky? And it's really no help to identify with the common people instead of the heroes, for they too serve a clear purpose, comic rather than tragic, and we're none of us in real life funny for long.

Meaning in life is not discovered in role or destiny. We manufacture it as constantly as the trees do oxygen, and it's often more useful to others than to ourselves, which may be a test of its validity.

True amateurs, we improvise in the moment for the moment a meal or a melody for ourselves at least, as often for others, and, unlike the fate of kings, such meanings are shared. As we multiply them among us almost without noticing, surely without undue attention, we make our lives possible. For we are really nourished by the likely, what we make, give, see each day, each season. This bucket of weeds, the ham defrosting on the drainboard, the washes of trout lilies in the woods define and illuminate our real lives.

# TAXING OUR PATIENCE

{ November 2001 }

The B.C. government's ideal citizen is a rich, rugged individualist whose only demand is a cut in taxes. Cuts in income tax can be designed for the greatest benefit to the rich and are therefore better than reductions in sales taxes, which would disproportionately benefit the poor. The rich will also suffer less from the reduction in services required as a result of tax cuts. They don't apply for welfare or take up space in home-less shelters. White-collar criminals rarely go to jail. The rich can pay for their own medication and go south of the border for medical help if they are impatient with waiting in line. If their children are particularly gifted or learning disabled, they can be sent to private school for the special attention given in

63

smaller classes. For the rich the ideal government is one which gets least in their way.

The rest of us, whether a single mother on welfare, a family with a mortgage, or an old age pensioner, are a nuisance, making demands on the government which involve increasing rather than cutting services in health, welfare, and education. Most of us would gladly forego tax cuts for a government which, in our name and with our money, would invest in the future of the province.

The government instead wants to persuade us that the institutions developed for our collective good are luxuries we must learn to pay for or do without. We are to be persuaded that what we have already collectively paid for must now be paid for again out of each of our pockets. Otherwise we are free loaders, feeding at the public trough, abusing the system. "Entitlement" is the word for a bad attitude. "Responsibility" is the key to good citizenship.

The catch is that, as a citizen, I can't be individually responsible for all the needs to be met for the young, the poor, the ill and the elderly. With my tax refund I can buy a new car or a cell phone, go out to dinner, take a trip, each of which might help to stimulate the economy in a small way but does nothing to improve the quality of life for those around me. I can't hire a teacher or a social worker or a nurse except for my own use. The only way I can support vitally important services is as a citizen paying taxes.

Of course we can and do fundraise and volunteer to support and improve schools, community centers, hospitals, but to be efficiently run and available to anyone, our institutions must be adequately funded by our tax dollars. Our health care isn't free. It's prepaid. If the government defaults, it is refusing to collect and spend our money on the services we require.

Double billing isn't the solution. It's a criminal offense that no double-talking will cover up. Only the rich can afford to be so duped, and how long will even those ideal citizens be willing to pay for the privilege? In the long run, a government survives by fairly taxing our income rather than our patience and good will.

# THE WELFARE OF CHILDREN

{ October 2001 }

The reason many Canadian children live in poverty is that children have become a luxury only the rich can afford. Once viable investments for a family who could expect to benefit from their labor throughout their lives, children could contribute by tending animals, gardening, harvesting, growing into the harder work of adolescence until they became adults to run the farm and tend those too old to work. Now there are few productive tasks for children in a family no longer engaged in agriculture, jobs for adolescents outside the family usually paying too little for the family to benefit. All that can be hoped of an adult is that he/she earns enough to pay taxes which support government-sponsored pensions for aging parents.

"I have spent more time with children than many people do."

Still, as a society we expect families to produce the next generation, to endure the financial drain they are through childhood, to provide for their education after high school so that the nation can benefit from a well-educated citizenry to keep our financial engine running, to ensure our country's health, wealth and wisdom into the future.

Because most families can't afford to raise and educate more than one or two children, our population is shrinking and proportionately growing older. Too many of those too few young are malnourished in childhood and deprived of the education they need to be productive citizens.

One answer to the problem has been immigration. Aside from the dubious morality of taking the best and brightest from countries greatly in need of them, we also tend to belittle and misuse their talents for the first generation, allowing foreign doctors to drive cabs, foreign nurses to clean toilets so that only their unaccented, Canadian-educated children can become really productive.

Only when we really understand that children are a financial burden to their families and the nation's greatest financial resource will we develop policies to ensure that we reap the benefit of their potential worth.

It is not in the nation's interest to have vast numbers of children malnourished. Children on welfare are malnourished, and their mothers have no hope of improving their lot without a good national day care system which would allow them to work.

It is not in the nation's interest to have vast numbers of young people under-educated. But children of the poor can't be expected to assume a fifty-thousand dollar debt for a college education.

This country should be profoundly grateful for those people willing to make the sacrifices involved in raising children, the altruism of their care and love. They should be supported in the work they are doing. For in a culture where children have become an unaffordable luxury, there is no future.

# OTHER PEOPLE'S CHILDREN

{ May 1998 }

I don't know where the boys, Jonathan, aged five, and Adam, aged six, learned about fishing, but they both became obsessed with the idea of catching a fish. Their bemused fathers, transplanted urban Englishmen, tried to placate the children with trips to the Aquarium. Jonathan and Adam didn't want to see fish; they wanted to catch them. Their fathers not only didn't know how, they had a real aversion to blood sports, having from childhood identified with the hunted, rejecting their own fathers' masculine enthusiasm for killing. They wanted to be gentle fathers to their own sons. Jonathan and Adam wanted to go fishing.

I learned both to fish and hunt as a child in the California wilderness. I was taught them as survival skills for putting meat on the table and protecting the orchards and vegetable garden. There were rules: never catch or kill more than you need; kill cleanly and quickly, and (because we weren't real pioneers) give your prey a sporting chance unless it is a physical threat to you. So we didn't fish with live bait or hunt deer with flashlights at night. Because we didn't have livestock, we scared bears away instead of shooting them.

I tried to explain the basic morality of such a childhood to Jonathan's and Adam's troubled fathers.

"Don't think of them as Englishmen in a pack, chasing after the hounds for one poor fox or hare. Think of them as Indians preparing for winter."

"Why don't they want to be bird watchers?"

I remembered a day in early adolescence when I realized I loved fishing mainly for long walks along the river bar, hunting for hours in the quiet orchard or silent woods. I learned the greater pleasure of going unencumbered by rod or rifle. I learned to enjoy the day empty-handed, to go home empty-handed unless I'd picked some wild berries.

"Once you know you can, you usually outgrow it," I explained.

"Maybe women do," they replied gloomily.

By misfortune, on a picnic outing up the Squamish road, we passed a sign advertising a trout pond where people could fish. Adam, already a reader, begged to stop, and Jonathan echoed his pleas. The fathers resolutely refused. Since I had been raised a fishing snob to hunt fish only in the wild, I couldn't muster the enthusiasm to side with the children, who took their revenge later on a river bank. They refused to collect interesting rocks and instead hurled them at fish they imagined swimming below the surface of the water, practically a harmless occupation, but the principle of it effectively offended their fathers.

I can't think now why I finally did agree to take the children back to that fish pond. I didn't by then own any rods or tackle, and perhaps it simply seemed easier and cheaper than organizing the real thing. It was a hot August day, and by the time we arrived the children were carsick and cranky. The pond was not attractive, a hole bulldozed in the earth filled with stagnant, scummy water. There was no one about, so I climbed to a trailer some way off in the bush and roused the drunken owner, who found me a couple of poles and told me I should pay two dollars for every fish we caught.

When I got back to the pond, Adam was sounding out the instructions written on various small signs around the pond.

"Why does it say 'Worm Pile'?" he asked.

"Because we have to dig worms for bait," I explained.

"Alive worms?" Jonathan asked.

"I'm afraid so."

"What does 'Dispatch Promptly' mean?" Adam asked.

"It means kill the fish quickly once you have caught it."

"Kill it?" Jonathan repeated in disbelief.

"If you want to take it home and eat it, you have to kill it," I said firmly.

"And pay for it too," Adam said, reading yet another sign.

I was sweating. There was no shade.

"Come on then," I said. "Let's dig for worms."

The boys were surprisingly squeamish about touching the worms, and there was no way either of them would thread a worm onto a hook. If live bait hadn't put me off as well, I might have insisted that fishermen had to bait their own hooks. I forced the wriggling worms onto the crude hooks while the boys made appropriately disgusted noises.

For a few minutes, because they could actually see the trout swimming around, the boys were mildly interested in holding their poles. I wondered what kind of dumb fish would take the bait with two small fishermen in such plain view. Jonathan trailed his hook out of the water to see if his worm was liking to swim. It was gone, so we had to repeat the grizzly business of impaling another.

"Be careful," Jonathan cried, "or you're going to kill him." Just as he dropped his hook back into the water, Adam's line jerked.

"What should I do?" he called. "What should I do?"

"Hang on tight and pull," I called back.

There was nothing to teach the boys about real fishing with crude poles without so much as a reel, no playing the fish to tire it, no net to scoop it out of the water. Adam simply dragged his catch out of the water and watched it flop in the dust. I picked up a rock and pounded it sharply on the head. Jonathan dropped his pole and burst into tears. Adam gave me a look no adult wants to see on a child's face.

"Now it has to be cleaned," I said, taking out my old fishing knife, the only sporting relic left from my childhood.

Both children moved off as far as they could get while I cut open the fish and gutted it. They made no protest when I took their poles and returned them to the drunk along with two dollars.

The fish in a plastic bag lay between the two boys on the back seat. Occasionally Adam stroked it.

"It has a pretty face," Jonathan ventured, by now recovered enough to feel a little jealous that he didn't have a fish of his own. "What's its name?"

As their fishing mentor, I should have told them you don't name what you have killed or may have to kill in the wild or the barnyard. It was knowledge that seemed as pointless as the afternoon.

Both fathers reported that the boys thought fishing was "okay," but they were reticent about the details and never asked to go again.

I thought, well, if they ever need to be put off anything else, I guess I'm their grownup, maybe when they get curious about shoplifting or drinking or girls or corporate management.

"Thank you," their fathers said. "Thank you very much."

# PEANUT BUTTER SUMMER

{ January 1994 }

Most of the summers of my childhood were spent at my maternal grandmother's two hundred and forty acres in the California redwoods on the South Fork of the Eel River, ten miles from the nearest town, Garberville. My older brother and I were the only children among aging adults, who were good for a card game or a story but had limited patience for our constant energy, gladly offering us the freedom of vineyard, garden, orchard, meadows and woods. We could fish but we couldn't boat or swim in the river without adult supervision. My brother, tiring easily of my company, would outdistance me on the river bar or lose me in the woods where I soon learned to find my own way and enjoy my solitude, picking fruit and berries, watching birds, chipmunks, skunks, deer, and even an occasional bear.

When we were living outside St. Louis, the war prevented our summer journey to California. I was disconsolate to have no escape from the long-established cliques in junior high and the neighborhood by whom I, as a new kid, was only marginally tolerated. Mother, facing the misery I would be at home for a long summer, suggested summer camp in the Ozark Mountains, but I didn't want to be marooned for two weeks with kids who already treated me badly, hiding my bike, stealing my lunch, whispering among themselves at my expense. Mother suggested that I go at a different time in the summer. I could swim and hike and have a real vacation from my taunting older brother and demanding little sister.

I did know it was a bad idea, but at eleven I was too proud to voice my real fears. I was a finicky eater, suffering a delusional fear of being poisoned by anything out of the ordinary, which included ice-cream sodas, all soups and casseroles, cooked vegetables and wild rice. Ever since at five I'd had to wear two-piece underwear because I was so tall for my age, I had been pathologically shy about undressing in front of anyone. I had never washed my own hair. My mother did not have to be told these things about me, and, though she was too kind a woman to send me off for the express purpose of poisoning and humiliating me, she might be excused for letting the thought cross her mind that camp might be good for me.

In fifty years, the vividness of my misery has faded a little, but I can still smell the one-room cabin that housed six musty campers and a counselor, and the three-hole doorless outhouse which I used only in the middle of each sleepless night. I ate so little that constipation wasn't a severe problem for some days.

I've been getting out of the wrong side of the bed and starting off on the wrong foot all my life, and by now I'm used to it. When I was eleven, I was skeptical, but I still invested some hope in new beginnings. The first day, my desire to pronounce the muddy pond too polluted to swim in was overcome by my desire to show off my swimming. I did win the first race, but I was disqualified because I didn't breathe with each stroke, something my champion swimmer father had taught me was unnecessary for sprints. That night, to comfort myself in my too short and narrow cot, I kept a large wad of forbidden bubble gum in my mouth and woke with it in my hair. It had to be cut out by my counselor. She had also been my sixth-grade teacher, the only person I had known before in the camp, so she was already aware of my social limitations.

She actually tried to be kind to me and enlisted the help of other campers to make me feel welcome by leaving little bouquets of wild flowers on my pillow, a square of chocolate at my place at the table, but, since I didn't know why these offerings were being made, I suspected a plot which would resolve into some exacted payment. There was something suspiciously smarmy about the whole place that made me very uncertain about how to watch my back. I wasn't used to not knowing who my enemies were.

I have always hated crafts. I am a perfectionist, and I knew even in kindergarten that lumpy clay ashtrays and pen wipers made lousy presents even for indulgent parents. Required to do something, I struggled at making a leather wallet for my father so thick he couldn't get it into his pocket.

I'd long before been put off group singing when I'd been asked by a music teacher to mouth the words rather than sing because my voice was so deep. Later I turned this limitation into a talent for lip syncing Danny Kaye records, but singing grace before meals and songs around the camp fire that summer I was simply a face-making mute.

At the end of the first endless week, when I was out of clean underwear, starving, constipated, and suffering from a nearly constant migraine headache, I approached a pair of visiting parents and offered them money to get me out of there. I must have been eloquent because, after a consultation with the counselors, I was allowed to leave. When my rescuers wouldn't accept my bribe or even let me pay for my own lunch, I spent my money on decent presents for the family. The only one I remember was a carton of Chesterfields for my father.

Mother couldn't resist, "Well, at least it's made you more appreciative of home." I'm sure it was at least a week before I complained about food, and I didn't once for the rest of the summer complain of being bored, the alternative still too vivid. Because my brother and his chums were out shooting up the neighborhood with their B.B. guns, the outdoors was uninviting. Sitting by the radio eating peanut butter sandwich after peanut butter sandwich was summer vacation enough for me until the war was over and I could go back to the wilderness solitude for which summer is intended, that sweet long parole from the prison populated by one's hideously similar peers.

# HOW THE WORLD WORKS

{ November 2006 }

Growing up, I never thought about earning a living, perhaps because most of the women I knew, except for school teachers, didn't. I didn't even think about earning money, though I did from time to time and couldn't think what to do with it. I wasn't without ambition. I wanted to be a doctor until I took chemistry and realized what a long, hard and often dull road it would be for me to do what I was already doing in my everyday life, keeping myself and those I cared about alive. The first job I was paid for was lifeguarding and teaching swimming at a summer day camp, wooing a few water-phobic children into the pool and saving others from their suicidal recklessness. It was not unlike my chores at home, keeping a much younger sister and her friends from playing in the street, keeping a drunken older brother away from the family car, guarding aging grandparents against falling. My other job, setting pins in a bowling alley, was more practical since it paid for my own games, and I had only myself to look out for, leaping away from balls pitched by homicidal bowlers. The other job my brother and I had at the alley was teaching newly-blind veterans of the South Pacific war to relearn their balance by bowling. We weren't paid for that. We didn't expect to be.

When I finished high school, I hired myself out as a supply typist at Stanford University, only to kill time waiting to be accepted there as a student. Sent from department to department wherever extra typing was needed, I inadvertently learned more than I wanted to know about how badly run an institution could be and still go on functioning from year to year, when by any reasonable calculation its walls should have come tumbling down. Assigned to type addresses on envelopes for a fundraising campaign, I went to work a second day to find every envelope I'd typed the day before torn in half on my desk, my triumphant boss pointing out that I had not looked up newly-assigned zip codes, an instruction I hadn't been given. For the moment outraged at the waste of my time and hers, I then thought I was being paid by the hour and it shouldn't matter to me what the result was. Typing orders for the Purchasing Department, I was bored enough to pay attention to details. We were instructed, for the purpose of keeping our desks clear, to throw away any orders left untyped at the end of the day. I soon discovered that departments were putting in duplicate orders in the hope that one or another might actually be sent. I pointed out one duplicate to my boss who growled, "You're paid to type." Then I found an order for live monkeys without a delivery date specified. Again the response was, "You're paid to type." The monkeys arrived on a Sunday and all died before they were discovered. I was blamed and transferred to the General Secretary's office, where I sat next to a young woman who had just graduated from Stanford with a degree in creative writing. The second week there, I typed my own rejection, signed the registrar's name, and quit. I wondered later what would have happened if I'd sent myself an acceptance, but by then I was convinced Stanford couldn't survive for another four years.

As an undergraduate at Mills College, I confined myself to volunteer work, first teaching handicapped children to swim at the YMCA, later working with them in the classroom. In the faculty lounge on breaks, I encountered a nearly universal cynical burnout in teachers who, whatever their initial motivation, were now only working for a living in a prison of exhaustion and defeat. I found the same punitive cynicism at Barnardo's Orphanage where I volunteered to run a recreation program once a week. When I protested the brutality inflicted on some of the children, I was not dismissed because I was not paid. Help was badly needed.

I remembered that freedom when I taught at a girls' boarding school in New England. There when I objected to anything, I was told, "You're paid to teach." By then, in my early twenties, it had finally dawned on me, with a little helpful prodding from my father, that, if I wasn't going to marry someone to take myself off my father's hands or learn to write for money, I was indeed going to have to work for a living, intermittently anyway, while I

"I gradually learned not to call myself a writer at all."

saved for time to write only what I pleased. Though living in at a boarding school allowed me to save much of my salary, I was too claustrophobic and demoralized to last more than two years.

For a time I tried mixing part-time work with writing, but, whether I was tutoring or marking papers or reading scripts for television, I was paid too poorly to survive. So again I found myself attached to a university, not as a lowly typist this time but as Assistant Director of International House at the University of British Columbia, where I was expected to coordinate student activities and promote involvement with the larger community.

What the job description didn't include was the supervising of the building of a new International House on campus, which should have been the architect's job, but he was killed in a mountain climbing accident soon after I was hired. I had no authority to consult the contractor nor any formal training for such a job, but my father was a builder. I knew how to read blueprints. I understood the basics of wiring and plumbing. While the students and I waited in a Quonset hut with little room for ambitious activities, I roamed the building site, chatting with various workers. That's how I discovered, four weeks before we were to occupy the new building, that it wasn't hooked up with the sewer system. I phoned Buildings and Grounds, to be told that International House was scheduled to be connected with a sewer extension planned for the Fisheries building, a federal project that was not yet even on the drawing board. "I'm to deal with hundreds of students in a building without flush toilets or running water?" I phoned the President, who had a particular interest in anything to do with foreign students. He discovered there was no budget for hooking up to a nonexistent sewer extension. The feds were supposed to pay. I suggested that Rotarians and other professional groups who had raised the money for the building might take a dim view of its standing idle for two years. Eleanor Roosevelt was already scheduled for a formal opening in six months' time. I don't know where the money came from, but the potential scandal was large enough for emergency measures. Bulldozers were on site the next week, and we moved in on schedule.

Other less dramatic financial problems were much more difficult to solve. The groups who raised funds for the building expected the university to pay operating expenses, which had been only very modestly allocated. Aside from my small salary, there was a token amount for a faculty member to be a token director, sitting in his handsome office for half a day a week, and a janitor. If the cafeteria was to function, pay for the cook had to come from profits. Though I was often out of the office for such events as the President's luncheons for visiting foreign dignitaries, or simply elsewhere in the building supervising one activity or another, I had no secretary to answer the phone, give out information or deal with routine mail. Aside from the students' modest membership fees, there was no money for equipment or programs. Yet International House was the new showcase on campus, and we were to be a model of interracial and international cooperation for not only the student body but the community at large.

An evening when the Vancouver Hungarian community and the Hungarian students were together sponsoring a musical evening, I had to provide two pianos. There was one beat up old upright in the music room which with much pleading I had persuaded Buildings and Grounds to paint, and I borrowed another practice piano very reluctantly lent by the music department. The day before the event, I arrived to find the painter already at work, painting the borrowed piano, an accident I later tried to pass off as an act of gratitude to the music department.

Less comic was the refusal of the university to allow me or appoint someone else to be student adviser to members of International House. In those unenlightened days of the late '50s, there were only two student advisers for UBC's ten thousand students, and international students were to have no special privileges. When a landlord phoned to complain that a foreign student was behind in his rent and hadn't been around for a couple of weeks, I called hospitals and the police, more often than not finding the missing student in a mental ward, still too new in the country to have concerned friends and thousands of miles away from family. It became a joke that anyone who survived the dark month of February without a trip to the hospital was insensitive. Many of the students were traumatized refugees from Eastern Europe, and nearly all, except for a few glamorous East Indian princes who came with servants to do their lab work, were very poor, often cold and hungry and lonely.

The vast majority of them were young men, many of them from cultures foreign to social dancing, which in those days was the principal means of meeting young women. I had no money to hire a dancing instructor but I finally found a volunteer willing to give lessons on a Sunday evening. When I asked for young women to come as partners, the Dean of Women objected, "No good Christian girl will dance with a foreigner, particularly on Sunday."

It was the Dean of Women who also insisted that all interior doors be equipped with windows so that it could be seen at a glance what was going on in the music room, the conference room, the library, even in my office. I also discovered moral police among board members who would drop into my office to report sighting a young black man holding hands with a young white woman in the lounge. The International House motto, "That Brotherhood Shall Prevail," did not mean that sort of fraternizing.

The students needed more reasonably-priced and better housing, summer jobs acceptable to the immigration authorities. I went to church prayer groups, had lunch with Rotarians and Lions, explaining that it wasn't enough to provide an education for foreign students. They had to survive and thrive among us for the experience to be valuable. Did they know that a Japanese pilot who volunteered to bomb Pearl Harbor had been an exchange student in Oregon? "I can't rent a room to a black student. We have to share the toilet." "Foreign students are too small for the jobs I have to offer." How did work throughout the rest of the world get done when no man under 5'10" was qualified to do it? Even when I found jobs, I had to clear them with Immigration who insisted students could only work at jobs related to and furthering their studies. I placed two geology students for the digging of the Deas Island tunnel. I booked my West Indian steel band in Vancouver nightclubs because one of the performers was a sociology student doing research on prostitutes. It was always harder to place non-white students since they were so easily spotted and reported for depriving Canadians of jobs. British Columbia, and therefore the university, had so white an image of itself that native Indian students were registered as foreign students at International House.

Even if there had been enough hours in the day, I couldn't have met the most basic needs of the students. No one in authority wanted to fix the fractured and chaotic financing because its inadequacy was a way of subverting programs the university had no real desire to pay for. Idealism in international relations cannot survive application. Institutions survive only by reflecting not changing basic attitudes. I resigned at the end of the year.

Like Stanford, UBC and International House still stand after all these years of dead monkeys and unconnected sewers because people are doing what they are paid to do, correcting very little,

taking what blame there must be, sure enough the boat is sink-
ing not to be tempted to rock it.

Yet people go on building with a delusion of survival that
transcends cynicism and inertia, not to be found entirely guilty
beyond reasonable doubt.

Years after I left the university, I was invited to a dinner party
at the Faculty Club, a building just up the road from International House, given to the university by Leon Koerner. He
chose the site and the architect, and he was the host of the party,
thanking people who had helped put on his niece's wedding. It
was an elaborate meal, roasted birds with their feathers restored,
a huge salmon embossed with the university crest, a great variety of wines. When we were all seated, just before we started the
meal, Leon Koerner stood to give a speech.

"The sun never sets on the British Empire," he began, not
well I thought.

"But it does set on British Columbia, and I have provided it
for you." He nodded to the waiters behind him who drew open
the curtains of the tall windows. The sun went down. I faintly
heard somewhere nearby a toilet flush.

# MUCH OBLIGED

{ February 1995 }

Parents seem to me kinder than they used to be about the jealousy a child feels toward a new addition to the family. They understand that the desire to feed the baby into the woodstove, bury it in the garden, send it back where it came from is not the murderous Cain suddenly manifest in their heretofore innocent two-year-old. Parents trying to accommodate the rage of that betrayed two-year-old will sometimes liken the experience to introducing a lover into the family. In our culture it's not a useful comparison, for such a rival is usually not long tolerated, and either the spouse or the lover goes. Children are expected to be, in the long run, wiser about and more tolerant of rivals. A more useful comparison would be with a harem, the members of which are forced to live together in competition for their master's attention. Some will always do whatever they can to maintain or achieve supremacy. Others, less confident of their charms or less ruthless, will make alliances among themselves to compensate for neglect. Such bondings of natural enemies are sometimes seen in our culture only after the fact, among ex-wives or ex-husbands who once experienced tyranny and betrayal at the same hands. It's a rare bunch of adults who voluntarily live together with a shared object of love.

What adults don't seem able to manage, we expect children to get used to, not because they are prisoners of a family and have no choice but because it is natural for them to learn to love their siblings.

Children recently in command of their bowels, trying out the new power of language, are not normally moved to protective tenderness for a thing helpless to do anything for itself yet able to command adult attention by a cry or a smell. A baby can't walk or talk or play. It has no charm to offset the power it has to use the very weapons a two-year-old has been urged to outgrow. To revert to screaming or wetting the bed no longer inspires sympathy.

It takes years, which are much longer for a child than for an adult, before a younger sibling can be any sort of companion. Most younger children will make the effort, never having had to give up the privileged state of only child, seeing older children along with parents as objects of power and possible love. But the wooing is harder against that barrier of fierce resentment and scorn.

Nearly my first memory as a child is standing in my crib in the dark rattling the bars of my cage to attract the attention of my older brother already asleep in his new youth's bed. He did not seem as aware of his new privilege as I was. He could get out of bed and come to play with me if he would. I roused a parent instead and, hearing those disapproving footsteps, I flopped down to feign sleep. My brother was roused and scolded for trying to disturb my rest. I was sorry for him but more relieved not to be caught.

Because my brother was naturally a more tactful and less volatile child than I, he got along better with most adults than I did. Neither of us wanted the sort of attention I did get from adults. He soon learned the privilege of being not only the firstborn but a boy, not so apt to be picked up and fondled. When you get the dime and your kid sister gets the kiss, both of you know which is the coin of the realm. He didn't want me to share the kiss, but I did want him to share the dime.

We were named for our parents, a little Arthur and Jane to manifest their love. We were to treat each other with the same affection and respect. But we hadn't fallen in love, chosen each other and taken vows of our own free will. Without reference to our needs and desires, we were dropped into the same prison of childhood to work it out as we could. I suspect the initial physical aversion and the good odds for incompatibility as much as any sexual taboo spares the children it does from incest. The physical intimacy which nourished our parents' relationship more often threatened ours. One's own body is bewildering enough to grow up in, its changing size and shape and smells often barely tolerable to ourselves. My brother and I learned to sit as far apart as we could on the back seat of the car, avoid each other's rooms, and were only really comfortable with each other out of doors.

"My brother and I were only really
comfortable with each other out of doors."

In fact, we managed best not only out of doors but cut off
from civilization altogether, as we were nearly every summer
which we spent on two hundred and forty acres of redwoods, a
few acres cleared for houses, barns, orchard, vineyard, and vegetable garden, ten miles from the nearest town. We usually went
our separate ways, Art to hike and hunt, I to forage for wild berries or simply to dream, but the river brought us into proximity
for swimming and fishing. We could spend a day on the river
fifty yards apart rarely exchanging a word. My brother says he's
never found another woman to go fishing with who can spend

the day making no claim on his attention, satisfied to be simply in the same neighborhood.

I did see it as a real and fragile privilege since in the world of school he hardly tolerated acknowledgement of our relationship. In that world I only wanted the political clout being his sister might bring. I was not any more interested in him than he was in me. The truce of those afternoons on the river was a rare defining of our relationship for ourselves, enough air and space around us for both of us to breathe freely.

By then we had a sister, eight years younger than I, ten years younger than Art, and we were escaping the mock-parental roles required of us. We didn't much resent the attention our parents gave her. I was grateful finally not to be the baby of the family, but I was more alarmed than my brother at the potential responsibility she could be to me. Perhaps he felt absolved for, having already tolerated the intrusion of one sister on his childhood, he could leave the chore of this new one to me.

Some siblings do learn to love each other quite early on. I wonder if they bond together sometimes against bad parenting or other hostile brothers and sisters. Peculiarly wise parents may help children away from the ruthless competition both the world and their own needs teach them. Or it's simply a happy accident that two people with a natural affinity are born into the same family. But most of us survive our growing up in a rhythm of battles and truces until we are allowed finally to go our separate ways, carrying the obligations of our blood with some ambivalence still.

The much smaller families most of us now grow up in and produce may lessen the traditional tensions and trials of childhood, but more and more children are being asked to adjust not only to their own siblings but to accept the children of a step-parent. Mixed families present political problems far more complex. The battles often go on longer, the truces are briefer, and the old wounds can ache in bad emotional weather for years.

Yet our most common expression for a long and abiding friendship is, "She's like a sister to me. He's like a brother." That dream of generous loyalty, uncomplicated by desire, survives our experience and becomes a metaphor for our most successful experiments in human relationship.

Though we have choices once we're free of childhood, they are neither as many nor as important as we are led to believe. The very choice of a mate immediately cancels or at least postpones other options. Friends are as often accidents of geography as the bonding of free spirits. The vast majority of people in our lives are fellow prisoners, beginning with our families, extending into the classroom and into work, casting back again into the families we choose to have with children we do not choose.

The long dependence of childhood teaches us what social creatures we have to be. Without the care and protection of others we would not survive. Neither would we without learning to negotiate with our rivals until we can come to an accommodation with them for our mutual good. Though the hope that we might like or even love those we have to live with survives, what we more basically learn is that it is not necessary to like or love to get along with other people in relative harmony. Liking and loving may even be beside the point, or more dangerously distract us from the true nature of obligation.

"Much obliged" is a response gone out of fashion, but it is both the simplest and truest expression of the condition in which we live, much obliged to all around us, and, if we know what we are about, much obliging as well, not out of friendship or passion but in kinship for our common good.

# AGAINST THOSE WHO WOULD FORGET

{ February 1995 }

Maybe the reason so many parents have amnesia about their own misadventures in childhood and adolescence is that their moral burden in raising children is so great they need to invent themselves afresh as untarnished souls worthy of the task. If your first break-and-enter took place when you were three-and-a-half, if you shoplifted for the first time when you were six, if you routinely filched change from the cracks in your father's armchair for movie money, if you smoked your first cigarette at eleven (which was, of course, stolen), and suffered your first drunk and hangover at twelve, who are you to tell any kid at whatever age how to behave? I understand the rationale for not confessing to such a past, for children would surely use it against you at crucial moral moments; yet not to remember inspires a self-righteousness repugnant to all young offenders, who take correction best from those who also understand them. Too, such amnesia is a source of what can be paralyzing fear, for if you don't claim your own less than perfect past, your children in their misdeeds can seem to you doomed monsters instead of young, only partially socialized, creatures on their way to as responsible and respectable an adult life as your own. Remembering can help you be kind in your firmness and infect even your sternest warnings with hope.

Do not mistake me. The criminality of children is not to be excused nor its real consequences dismissed. I probably would not have remembered my break-and-enter job at three-and-a-half if my father hadn't taken time to discuss it with my five-year-old brother and me. Instead of taking us swimming the next day, he joined other young fathers in the neighborhood to repair the damage half a dozen of us had done. We had been in pursuit of candy rumored to be stored in the attached garage of a house left vacant by vacationing neighbors. We were children who played together often under the supervision mainly of maids. Our Josephine was a tyrant, and there was never any mischief when she was in charge, not much fun either since she punished on suspicion rather than proof. But on Josephine's day off, when we were all under Rose's eye, nothing we could think up to do could compete with her fascination with movie magazines. Eating out of the neighbors' garbage cans, playing doctor under the card table, losing Jerry in the woods, and finally even breaking into that house couldn't attract her attention. Our strategy was to tear our way into the back screen porch, then break the window in the back door and search the house for a key to the garage. I never got into the house. I stopped to play with toys on the porch. If there was any candy, nobody found it. Only some hours later when the damage was noticed did sightings of us through the afternoon link us with the crime.

Because we hadn't actually been seen doing the deed, our father asked us if we had been involved. My brother, left to himself, might have hedged but, bound to a younger sister with a passion for telling the truth, he confessed before I could beat him to it, not because I was motivated by any moral superiority but by a more reckless sense of drama. Once we had confessed, Mother thought the discussion should be broadened a little to include not only the break-and-enter but other behaviors that had also been noticed by adult spies when we were under Rose's blind eye. Before the session was over, my brother had promised not to eat out of garbage cans. I was too finicky about food ever to have been tempted or even bullied into such gluttony, but I had to promise, in my turn, not to lose Jerry in the woods again. He was even younger than I and often a burden to us. We'd apparently been too discrete about playing doctor for that to have come under scrutiny. Rose wasn't fired, but I don't remember being sent to her care again. Probably Mother took over on Josephine's day off. With Mother there was reading aloud, singing while she played the piano, baking cookies, which beat scrounging in garbage cans and breaking into houses for fabled treats.

It's a rare child who hasn't shoplifted at one time or another. Even very small children know it is wrong, but they don't distinguish as much as adults do between swiping an extra piece of candy out of grandmother's box on the piano and robbing a store. Degrees of villainy have to be taught, just as we learned what for us seemed a rather arbitrary distinction between taking the spare change that had fallen out of Dad's pockets into his chair and the money in Mother's purse. The one was really fair game, the other a major crime.

The moralities we teach children aren't always entirely rational on close examination. Some behaviors have to be learned like irregular verbs, by rote rather than logic. Just as a parent has to say over and over again, "Taught not teached," so in matters of small change and sweets, lessons have to be repeated.

While it is hard and repetitive work to teach children to respect other people's property, it is not as frustrating as refereeing wars over their own possessions. How easy it is to become impatient with a two-year-old who snatches the rattle out of a baby sibling's hand or with a four-year-old's raging refusal to be generous or even fair over the sharing of toys not only with siblings but with friends. The problem is that children perceive very early the rules which apply only to them and resent the double standard. I might have to be the last one on the block to ride in my new pedal car, but I don't see the neighbors taking turns driving Dad's new Ford. My craft box is supposed to be open to anybody who wants to mess around in it, but Mother's sewing cabinet is off limits even to Dad. A lot of the horror stories told by people who do remember childhood have to do with being humiliated into "sharing," which was too often giving up a favorite doll to an aggrieved sister, a demanding friend, or even to the poor, the returning of "stolen goods" to another child, a grandparent, a store. You were supposed to share or even give up anything to which you felt some claim to anyone who wanted it, but to take what you wanted was stealing.

I might have been four when half a dozen of us cousins helped ourselves to a bagful of corn from Farmer Brown's field and then tried to roast it over an open fire. Our grandmother spotted the smoke and came after us, not breaking her stride as she snapped a switch from the apple tree on her way. My brother and I saw her in time to scramble free, with the presence of mind to take half a dozen ears of corn with us. But our cousins, in Grandmother's care for the day, were not so lucky. We could hear their cries as we disappeared into the safety of our own house across the street. That night at dinner when we were having our first whole ear of corn each, my mother looked at me and asked, "Did Farmer Brown really give you this corn?" My brother, whose explanation it had been, gave me a warning look. "He has lots," I said, "he should share." My mother raised an eyebrow to my father, who made no comment.

Though parents berate themselves whenever children, left to their own devices, get into trouble, some lessons are more quickly learned by experience. After my early run-in with rum and coke, I drink coke straight to this day. And after, on a dare, smoking a cigar in the back row of a movie house and then fainting dead away, I have had only one or two cigars since, and I haven't smoked them seriously. You don't always have to be caught to be sorry. Sometimes a terrified parent punishes a child who might otherwise have burned itself and therefore simply postpones the lesson only the stove itself can teach. But neither parent nor child is easily reconciled to such cause and effect. The burned or broken child will wail, "Why did you let me do it?" And even if parents can remember the efficacy of their own hard lessons, it's not much comfort. But gradually giving up omnipotence is what parents have to do to prepare for their offsprings' adolescence.

Surely you must be able to remember the awful revelation that your mother didn't know what you were supposed to wear, how you were supposed to talk, what you were supposed to think. Suddenly even the dumbest kid in the class knew more about the real world than your mother did. My own father missed that fall from grace. He was away at war. My mother was better than most because she did remember hating what her mother wanted her to wear. But she stayed sticky about four-letter words, mostly for my father's sake, I think. He said we couldn't use them or even respond to them unless someone called us a "son of a bitch" which was an insult to our mother; then we could beat them to a bloody pulp. I have been called all kinds of names in my time, but I have waited in vain for that magic permission to demolish my enemy. About *how* to think, my mother did as much talking back as we did, and she didn't always lose. We tried to go on scorning her ignorance by keeping her in ignorance of much that we thought and did.

I had decided to smoke, but I didn't want to make a fool of myself by trying it for the first time in front of my friends. I practiced at night after Mother had gone to bed, flicking the ashes out a small hole in the screen of my bedroom window. One night, as I quietly lifted the window, I saw a small ashtray tucked between the sill and the screen.

Confrontation may sometimes be less effective than a tactful, even funny, gesture which allows the culprit to suffer discovery

The Rule family at South Fork, Jane second from right.

and embarrassment alone. My mother didn't have to make me admit to her as long as I admitted to myself that she was, after all, not born yesterday.

My father came home after three years at war to children he no longer knew. In our teens even the most benign authority threatened the freedom we had won from our mother. Our parents had never succumbed to the divide-and-conquer strategies that children often find such successful weapons, but in those first months of readjustment, though they never disagreed in our presence, I am sure Mother often was our advocate behind their bedroom door. Mother was more of a pragmatist than Dad. With the benefit of those hard war years, she had come to the view that she couldn't finally tell us what to do, only attempt to influence our choices with reason and love. Dad, on the other hand, thought our choices should still be limited. Bottom lines should be set about school attendance, weekend curfews, domestic chores. My brother suffered both Dad's absence and presence more than I did. But we both resented the implication that we had taken advantage of our mother during those years when we should have been a great deal more help. Neither of us had accepted as uncritically as our mother did his abdication of the family for the higher good of serving his country. We were proud of him, of course, a war hero in our eyes when most of the other fathers we knew had stayed at home and made money. But if anyone had taken advantage of our mother, left her with too great a responsibility and not enough help, it was our father. She didn't let us complain to her, and we hadn't the courage to confront him, not out of fear of him so much as out of some regressive need for his authority. We weren't old enough to dare to win that basic battle.

I sometimes think that gap of three years didn't leave us so much with unfinished business as with a sad nostalgia. I remember the resignation in my father's voice when he said, "You're now climbing trees too high for me to get you down." I didn't know then that there would be times in my life when I wished he could.

A pregnant friend once asked my mother when you started letting your children go. "When they're born," she replied. In much of adult living we can avoid being reminded of how hard and humiliating to our self-esteem it is to share what we need and what we love, much less to give it away. Most of us pay our taxes grumblingly and volunteer to share or give away only what is superfluous by our own definition and at our own whim. Then we face the needs of children, teaching them those hard lessons we have tried to forget for ourselves, sharing what is most precious to us, and letting them go.

# THINGS

{ April 2003 }

In a culture where everything we need or want has been mass-produced and commodified—food, clothing, shelter, entertainment, art—we celebrate our freedom from what was once, and still is in many parts of the world, the all-consuming and often overwhelming task of daily survival. What we dedicate ourselves to instead is earning the money which will provide us with the basic necessities and, if we are fortunate, the luxuries which make life not only possible but comfortable and nourishing to both body and spirit. If we raise some of our own food, it is for the pleasure of working the earth, watching and encouraging growth, not because we would otherwise go hungry. If we make some of our own clothes, we do it to free ourselves of conventional styling, express an individuality, not because we would otherwise go naked. If we entertain ourselves at all, make our own music, paint our own pictures, tell our own stories, it is not because we would otherwise do without, for there are those with gifts enough to entertain us professionally so that there is no real need to learn to play an instrument, sing, act, paint, write. Indeed, except for those few who have learned to make a business of a gift, there isn't time in our work-driven lives to develop those survival skills common and necessary to our ancestors.

If we sometimes, under the pressure and strain of our money-making, feel nostalgia for a life simpler and more basically necessary, we spend a couple of weeks in the wilderness or take a night course in rug making or sing our own carols. Except for the most obsessive, such activities are fads. Our cupboards and basements are filled with castoff bread pans, looms, boxes of wool and embroidery cotton, fishing tackle, wood-working tools, musical instruments, all the discarded detritus of our attempts to distract ourselves from our real lives, money- and time-bound, endlessly rich in everything we do not need to make and can easily buy.

Things mass-produced and impersonal so easily come by are also easy to get rid of. We trade in or dump most of the things we own without a moment's regret. In the California desert, houses are routinely sold with all their contents, even to the bed linen, pictures on the wall, books on the shelf. People move on with nothing but their latest clothes and perhaps a few bits of jewelry, choosing to live as refugees have been forced to, traveling away from the prison of land, of home, of things, free of the obligations of the past, of the traditions of survival, hermit crabs ready to occupy whatever castoff shell takes their fancy.

My parents were nomadic, following my father's work from California to Illinois to Missouri until the war sent him overseas and settled his wife and children in California for the duration. Before each move, my mother had a sale which often, against our protests, included our recent Christmas presents of ping-pong table or pedal car, but our basic furniture did go with us, along with Mother's grand piano, pictures and family china. Those things did make whatever new house we moved into look a bit like home, even though what hadn't been given away or sold was often broken in the move.

Against that transient life were set the places of my mother's California childhood, still inhabited by grandparents, aunts and uncles. There was the Eureka house built by my great-grandfather, the summer house at Carlotta reached by a spur of the railway from Eureka to carry guests for weekend parties, and South Fork, a camp in two hundred and forty acres of redwoods where the family went by buckboard for a couple of weeks in the summer.

Wherever in the country we moved, we returned for the summer to South Fork. We lived in a redwood cabin with a wraparound porch. In my childhood there was no electricity, and we were ten miles from the nearest town. We were dependent on a vegetable garden, vineyard and orchard for fruit and vegetables. We fished for trout in the river, hunted rabbit, pigeon and deer for our meat. In the daylight hours we boated and swam and hiked. At night for entertainment there was an old wind-up Victrola from my great-grandmother's era, hesitation waltzes and

South Fork, Grandmother's summer
"camp in two hundred and forty acres of redwoods."

Harry Lauder songs, and there was a trunk of old clothes, dusters and flowered hats for dressing up.

At least once a summer my great-aunt would take me back with her to Carlotta, a much more civilized place where there was electricity. There were two kitchen maids and farmhands who brought fresh milk and eggs up from the barn every morning, along with fruits and vegetables from the garden and orchard. The women of the family were free of basic work to cultivate an acre of flower gardens, to cook only the fancier dishes while supervising the baking and bottling and cheese making. There was a quilting frame set up in the parlor where the women sat every evening, stitching and gossiping, and there were always bags of handwork, knitting, embroidery, needlepoint, crafts the girl children were expected to learn, each of us with a sampler.

Great-grandmother Jane Vance,
for whom Jane was named.

There were more exotic crafts. My great-grandmother wrapped her own fishing rods with bright silk thread, designed and tied her own flies. The men carved and made furniture. The women painted china. Nearly everything in the house at Carlotta had a personal history, tied not only to the person who made it but to the time it was made: the summer Great-grandmother shot the bear, the winter Charlie broke his leg.

Even at South Fork, the summer camp, the sheets on the beds were monogrammed, the pictures painted by members of the family, and in the small living room, a collection of Indian baskets hung on the wall, collected by my great-grandmother, who often traded her catch of trout for baskets from the Indians then still encamped on the banks of the river.

After the summer in the wilderness, I returned to whatever suburbia, blinking at electric lights, my feet uncomfortable in shoes, the things of a nearly forgotten bedroom unfamiliar and impersonal. I daydreamed of staying on at South Fork, crossing the river every day to take a county school bus to a rural school, learning the seasons of the river and the woods. But I was only a summer child, cast back into my mother's childhood for two or three months of the year, learning skills that had nothing to do with the suburban school yard, the traffic-filled streets, the stores full of things.

When war came and there was no gas to drive the two hundred and fifty miles to the redwoods, I learned to work for money in the summer, first teaching swimming, later typing in an office, clerking in a gift shop. I was not used to spending money, and I never felt the satisfaction I had when I brought a basket of apples from the orchard, a pail of berries from the field, a sack of corn I'd shucked just before dinner in the garden.

After the war when I was eighteen, South Fork was sold, so that my father could go into business for himself, settle in one place, and be his own boss. I went to Europe the next summer and never went home again for longer than a few weeks, busy as I was making my own way in the world, traveling light, earning money to buy time to be free of earning money, leery of the burden of things which couldn't be easily discarded and replaced, my most cherished possession a seven-pound portable typewriter, hand luggage on a plane and easily strapped onto a bicycle.

I traveled to great cities, studied in libraries and museums, went to theatres and art galleries. I wasn't very comfortable in great houses with their centuries of collections of furniture, china, paintings, great warehouses of personal belongings abandoned to public curiosity. Sometimes I escaped into the countryside where I found the hard, traditional life of peasants, still eking out a subsistence from their gardens and orchards, aloof from time, and occasionally I could make use of some of my nearly forgotten childhood skills, helping to bring in a harvest, churn butter, shell nuts, fish, but I knew I was even more an outlander than I had been as a summer child. I no more wanted that hard, simple life than I wanted a great house full of furniture.

I wanted to write but not what was timely and commercial and might therefore earn me a modest living. To support myself I became a teacher, a portable enough profession to let me keep moving, with summers and sometimes even with years off to write.

I was slower than most people I knew to move from furnished digs to unfurnished apartments to a home of my own, persuaded only when I realized I could leave a house of my own with its accumulated things and travel light again. A house could be more an anchor than a prison, and so mine became, furnished in good part by family castoffs, a grandmother's chair, refrigerator, and flat silver, a great-aunt's hope chest and china. I bought mainly beds and paintings. I have actually moved only three times in the last fifty years, though I have traveled widely.

Unlike my mother I have had only one garage sale in that time, when I moved from the big house in Vancouver to this house on Galiano which I'd already furnished. Then, nearly thirty years ago now, there were numerous young people who needed beds and chairs and dishes and bookcases so that they could furnish their lives with my castoffs. My parents, in old age, managed to reduce themselves to a three-room apartment in senior housing, only a little cramped by my mother's grand piano. I cannot think, as I look around me, how I might manage to do the same. I realize that I, instead of shedding my past as they periodically did, have accumulated it around me, and there is nearly nothing in this house which I could easily part with.

I have the Indian baskets which once belonged to my great-grandmother. I even have her old crank-up Victrola and some of her heavy, one-sided records. One of her fishing rods hangs on a wall in the garage. I serve tea in my mother's unmatching engagement cups. There are family chairs covered with needle-point designed by my father, executed by my mother, a rug they tied together. Then there are the things I've collected in my travels, my books and paintings. Even in my closets there are clothes I can't part with, things my sister designed for me, needle-point vests by my parents, a cloak I once bought for my mother in England. There is the jewelry I hardly ever wear, much of it trophies of great-aunts' long-ago love affairs.

I thank anyone who breaks a plate or a glass and am grate-ful to those who don't remember to return books. I give to any member of the family or any friend whatever they admire. It's not that I'm possessive of much that I own, more that I feel re-quired to give them a home or find another for them where the stories that surround them can be told again, where new stories might be attracted to or by them.

What I cling to is the refuse of lives now over in an ambivalence of grief and love, resentful that objects outlast those who have made them, found them, used them in daily life. I was taught and always intended to be a light traveler without the silly status of too many belongings, free equally of the basic chores of survival and burdens of ownership, to work, to travel, to write. How is it that I have now so much, too much, to show for it? I've long since written the large stories that were mine to imagine. What remains are the little stories all around me, hundreds of them. Things.

# MONEY

{ July 2001 }

Money in my childhood was as much a moral mystery as sex, only its superficial transactions visible to us with the milkman at the back door, the clerk behind the counter in a shop, or the attendant at the gas station. We were sometimes given chocolate money or allowed to play with the change from our father's pocket, but the women in the family inclined to think real money was dirty, would give us impetigo or worse. One great-aunt washed her bills, and they always smelled of her perfume when they dropped out of birthday cards. Sometimes we were allowed to spend gift money, not on frivolous things like candy or the movies but on a book or educational game. Often money we received went into a piggy bank and finally into a grownup bank downtown to be kept for the distant needs of our majority, in my brother's case an education, in mine a trousseau.

Our weekly allowance was ours to squander or save as we chose. I hoarded mine, often having to offer it up to my mother to pay the paper boy or laundress. My brother bought jaw-breakers and big/little books. I did not learn his ways. I liked the feeling of being able to help my mother out of grownup trouble. The other pleasure of money was treating my friends when the Good Humor truck came into the neighborhood. Later I used it to buy my way into my brother's clubs where I would otherwise be unwelcome. Once I bought a box of candles for him which came close to burning down a neighbor's house.

"I don't know where she got the money," my mother said. "She always seems to have money."

It was a major crime to look into our mother's purse for any reason, but the change that fell out of our father's pockets into the cracks of his big chair was fair game. We often found enough for an extra afternoon at the movies.

The only moneys we ever stole—misappropriated more accurately—were the dimes our parents gave us for the collection plate at Sunday School. We skipped out after the church service before the collection was taken in the classroom and spent those dimes on cokes at the drug store.

We were never paid by our parents to do chores. Except for making our beds, tidying our rooms, washing dishes, feeding the cat, and emptying waste baskets, later mowing lawns, washing cars, and looking after our much younger sister, I don't remember any great burden of work. Other tasks, handwork, gardening, picking fruits and vegetables, were presented as pleasures like fishing, hunting, swimming, hiking. If you decided you didn't like picking berries or walking logs across the creek, you were left to your choices.

We were never bribed to do anything by our parents, and punishment for failing to do what we were told never deprived of us of our allowance. We might be forbidden to play outside or sent to our rooms.

Our parents taught us no monetary causes and effects. Money was not allowed to talk. I don't think it was a moral principle. They instinctively sheltered us from the meanings of money as they did from hunger and cold, brutality of any sort they could keep out of our lives.

In our childhood of plenty, always protected from important want, our parents paid a kind of servitude for our comfort. They themselves were children who had always been and still were being bribed and punished by their parents. My father worked for his father and was given a house to live in. My mother was sent money by her parents to travel home for summers which she and my father couldn't otherwise afford. The Depression finally freed my father to seek his own way in the world but, through my mother, he was still bound by the controlling generosity of his in-laws who could provide much that he could not.

I was seven before I fell into my grandmother's first bribery trap. I wanted weekly riding lessons from an Indian fellow who ran a pony ring out on the highway. My grandmother offered to pay if I'd also take tap-dancing lessons. I hated them. I sat on the curb and cried after every lesson before I bicycled home. I didn't confide in my mother, already sensing how many hard bargains she'd had to make with her mother, but I did complain to my Indian friend, who immediately offered me a job helping to clean out his stable in exchange for my weekly ride. My grandmother was outraged. She tried to make my mother forbid me to do the work. But Mother refused. My grandmother then threatened to send me to private school. This time my father refused.

"I don't want her with children who have a great deal more than she has."

"You don't worry about what she's learning from all the children who have a lot less?"

Mother gave us enough extra sandwiches and cookies in our lunches to share with hungry friends. She fed the children we brought home from school, sometimes bathed them and sent them home in our outgrown clothes. She occasionally persuaded her parents to buy shoes not only for us but for the kids next door. Many of our friends had fathers out of work or parents who worked in the fields.

Every summer we went with my mother's parents to their summer home in the redwoods. Our own house was rented. I never knew where Dad stayed. He drove the two hundred and fifty miles to see us every weekend he could and spent his two-week vacation with us, fishing and swimming in the river. Mother cooked and cleaned and preserved vegetables and fruit, a maid of all work, while her parents played cards, read, and complained about us running wild in the woods and orchards, on the river. If we bridled at their nagging, Mother said, "They are giving us our summer vacation."

In the grownup world, those without enough money paid with themselves, in service, in obedience, in cheerful appreciation. Those with money conferred their favors as they chose, exacting what dependence suited them. Having money was not necessarily the result of working for it. My grandfather was a retired army officer on a pension, but the real money was Grandmother's money, something my father explained as "family money."

Grandmother had inherited real estate, stocks and bonds from her father and mother, then from a childless sister. Her only brother, who was blind and had never worked, looked after the real estate. The bank was in charge of her investments. She questioned neither. Her only requirement was having enough in her checking account so that she never had to balance it and could spend money on a whim. My father hadn't a high opinion of either Uncle Harry or the bank, but he neither interfered nor advised because as a son-in-law it was not his place. Mother, as a woman, was not expected to understand such matters. I learned from my father that, though Grandmother was not a very good steward of her money, she was properly generous to the family.

I was twelve when my father went off to war, and at that time he finally agreed that I could go to private school, perhaps in part because I qualified for a serviceman's daughter's scholarship. Grandmother didn't take over the financial burden of my education until I went to college, the first female to go on either side of the family. Grandmother was more interested in the clothes I would need than the books I would have to buy. After years of having nothing much more than school uniforms, a party dress or two and wilderness clothes for the summer, I suddenly had a closet full of skirts and sweaters of all colors, cocktail dresses, evening dresses, jackets, coats, shoes, even a hat or two, and Grandmother, who no longer went out into the world, took enormous vicarious pleasure in my wardrobe. When she read about a ball to be held at my college, she sent me a check to buy a new dress for it. She told me she'd never send another if I dared deposit it in my savings account. The next check I cashed at the local liquor store, and she made no comment.

"Why don't you apply for a scholarship?" she demanded, irritated by some gesture of independence.

"You can afford to pay for me. If I took a scholarship, one of my friends might have to drop out."

"Awfully moral and generous with my money," she said.

I do think she never threatened to withhold my tuition because she knew I could get a scholarship. It was Mother who heard her bitter complaints that I was not being social enough, that so much studying would ruin my health along with my chances for a good marriage.

"Men don't like women who are smarter than they are," Grandmother said.

But my father always said with pride that Mother had a better business sense than he did.

In fact, my grandmother and I liked sparring with each other, and she sometimes even lost with some grace.

For my twenty-first birthday she offered me her large opal ring, a car, a house, and I said to each, "Fine. I'll sell it." I wanted a year in England to study and write my first novel.

"All you ever think about is money!" she shouted on the phone.

At my birthday dinner, her dining room table was awash in small change. A piggy bank on a pedestal replaced a handsome

arrangement of flowers, and Grandmother had a toy cash register instead of a bell to ring for the maid. When she rang, all the
members of the family had been instructed to scoop up change
and put it in the piggy bank. Place cards were decorated with silver dollars. At my place was a fan made of paper dollars from my
brother, a camellia corsage backed with dollar bills from my sister, a framed hundred dollar bill from my parents. On the cake,
in which were hidden numbers of dimes, was written, "Money
Happy Returns of the Day." The birthday card she handed me
was an IOU for a monthly allowance to live in England for a year.

That night I lay on the bed in my college room, ferreting out
every last penny from that piggy bank until I was covered in
small change.

I shared a cold-water flat in London with an English friend.
I was almost always cold, occasionally hungry, and would have
been in worse trouble without the care packages from home to
supplement the rationed food of postwar England. I had never
kept house, shopped for food, or cooked. I hadn't even had a
clothes allowance in college. Since I'd first jingled coins in my
pocket, I had never bought anything more serious for myself
than toothpaste and shampoo. We didn't eat well, but we ate
better than most of our student friends because we had a stove
rather than a simple hot plate. We had no fridge but most of the
year the kitchen was cold enough to keep things from spoiling.

I learned to line up for cheap theatre tickets in the gods, to
find bargains in second-hand bookshops, and to take advantage
of all the museums, galleries, and libraries freely accessible to
everyone. I went to lectures, and I wrote my first novel, admiring
the chilblains on my knuckles as badges of my poverty. But that

year was a challenge and adventure because I didn't see it as the measure of the rest of my life. On the other side of the ocean there were still ice cubes, central heating, and steaks.

I came home from the year abroad to a financial confrontation. My father said that if I wanted to go on writing I would have to live at home. If I wanted to be independent, I would have to earn my own living. It was a reality that shocked us both. He had imagined turning me over to a husband who would care for me. I simply hadn't thought beyond being somewhere where I could write, but certainly I had not imagined ever going home again. I was twenty-two years old.

I wasn't afraid of work. During the war, when we couldn't get gas to go to the redwoods, I taught swimming at summer camp, set pins in a bowling alley, worked as a supply typist at a university, clerked in a gift shop. But none of that work provided a living wage. The first job I took didn't either, teaching in a girls' private school in New England, but I agreed to live in so that I could save most of my salary to spend the summer writing in England.

It was my first experience as a wage slave, nearly all my waking hours at the disposal of one boss or another, the head of the English department who dictated my teaching hours, the head of the biology department for whom I was a lab assistant, the head of the boarding department under whom I ran one of the three boarding houses. I not only taught, supervised study halls, ate and slept with the students, I organized field trips, dealt with parents, tended live animals in the lab at night, marked papers and planned courses in the early hours of the morning. I had a couple of evenings off a week, one full weekend a month. I wrote not a word and wondered how that writer self could survive the prison of the working world for $2,700 a year and room and board. I did hoard my earnings to buy two and a half months of freedom in England, but I was too demoralized to make much creative use of that time, the sentence, or another year's teaching, facing me in September.

I watched as most of my friends opted for marriage instead, but that choice seemed to me as much of a trap, if smaller, to be in service to the aspirations of a mate and soon the needs of children, as all-consuming as earning a living, perhaps in the end worse, to be bought for love rather than money. I chose instead to join my life with another independent woman, making her teaching way in the world.

Even with her help it took me ten years to develop a strategy for survival. I knew from the beginning that I would not earn my living as a writer if I was to stay free to write what was important to me. Writing had to be an avocation for which I must somehow pay. I looked for part-time work, for better-paid work, a contradiction in terms. I marked papers, read TV scripts, did freelance radio broadcasting, tutored, and saw my time devoured, my bank account diminished even by my very frugal living. I did write, though without publishing anything in those ten years.

Money for me was time, and I could measure anything, from a bottle of Scotch or a new shirt to a holiday trip, in the hours lost at my desk.

More important than single expenditures was overhead. We bought a house with mortgage payments less than the rent we'd been paying, with a student room we could let, providing income that covered our utilities. We bought nothing on time. With limited living expenses, I could finally work full-time at a decent wage every other year and take every other year for my own work.

When my writing began to be accepted for publication, I invested the money. The gradual accumulation of published work made me eligible for grants which bought more time to write. A small inheritance paid off our mortgage, and gradually money became a less all-consuming problem. We could travel, entertain, buy an occasional painting, but we were careful to stay debt-free, to keep monthly expenses low.

I did very occasionally write to make money. Once when we wanted to take a holiday in San Francisco for which we didn't have the cash, I spent one afternoon writing a short-short story for *Redbook* and was paid $1,000 for it, the same amount I had just received as an advance on a novel which had taken me two years to write. I felt neither angry nor discouraged, reaffirmed rather that what the world valued and what I valued were so far apart I could never be threatened by money defining the worth of what I did. When my papers sold to the university for far more than I'd ever been paid for publishing my work, I felt the same amused freedom. Money is time. If my waste paper can buy time to write a couple of books, who am I to quarrel?

At forty-five, I was finally making enough money writing to give up other work, except for handling investments of extra money. I had studied the stock market and for several years did the homework necessary to invest knowledgeably in Canadian companies, but it was a time-consuming business which bored me. I did not want to turn over extra funds to a stockbroker or banker as women in my family had done. I wanted to be responsible for managing what I earned.

120

When we moved to the little island of Galiano, I found an economy of a size I could understand and contribute to. Over the last twenty-five years, with my own money and some that I have inherited, I have invested in mortgages of the sort banks turn down, for young families, single mothers, retired couples. I've invested in local businesses with loans to a portable sawmill, a gift shop, a music company, a film school, a bakery, a cleaning company, a travel agent. In the process of being an unofficial bank on Galiano, I have talked frankly with all kinds of people about money, a prison of debt or an avenue of freedom, a mockery of self-worth or irrelevant to it, a power to control or set free.

I like to ponder about what money means, where it comes from, how it is used individually, communally, by governments. I like to try to understand how our attitudes toward it are developed, how much we are nearly mindlessly influenced by habits of family and culture, how little opportunity we take to talk with each other about the meanings of miserliness, generosity, charity, gambling. We seem so little confident about what we think and do about money that we're hardly willing to admit either how we get it or what we do with it.

The most money I ever made as a wage was from the six nights I worked as a change girl at Harold's Club in Reno, as part of my research for a novel I wanted to write. The hourly wage, the generous tips, and an employee's draw I won earned me more than any academic post I ever held.

I didn't like watching people lose money gambling. I don't buy lottery tickets or take long shots on the stock market. I am morally offended to see the bulk of the world's capital in the crapshoot of the money markets, doing nothing but multiplying or diminishing itself, creating no product, producing no jobs.

Yet everything to do with money is a gamble, buying a house, investing in a business or putting a child through college. What is worth gambling on, even at the risk of loss? Anything purchased can turn out to be a bad idea, from an overripe pineapple to a lemon of a car. Some of us deny the risk; others enjoy it.

The value of money is arbitrary and subjective. Our relationship to it is confusing and complex. My lawyer advises me that it is unwise to talk about it even now when the task left to me is willing it away. Maybe I should pass on my grandmother's birthday wish by signing off my will, "Money Happy Returns of the Day." Never mind the dimes in the cake are hard on the teeth.

Money does talk, and, if we are to say anything of value with it, we need to understand its basic grammar and teach it to our children so that we and they don't, in ignorance, get trapped in any of its many dependent clauses.

# GIVERS ANONYMOUS?

{ Undated }

A lot has been written about impulsive buy-
ing, that human frailty on which everyone from the corner gro-
cer to the multinational corporation depends for survival. Less
has been said about impulsive giving, inspired by the reckless
guilt we feel for our habitual and random greed. Organized
charities have arranged it so that we can give with the same card
we use for spending. So there on the list of dinners out, new
shoes, cameras, and plane tickets, occasional good deeds may
be found for the United Way or the United Nations. For most
of us there is no more rhyme or reason to our giving than to our
getting. The credit card account makes only one thing clear: we
get a lot more than we give.

Budgets for spending are usually made out to guard us against our impulses, to save money. When I made out a budget and discovered that eighty percent of what I called food was, in fact, liquid of one sort or another, I was too mortified ever to do it again. I think instead about the generous tax I pay for so many other people's benefit. At least seventy percent of that cost can be shifted over to the budget I make for giving, which is an exercise not for saving money but for increasing my generosity as well as making it more rational.

Before I had a budget for giving, my decisions were easier. I usually threw away any request that arrived after the fifteenth of the month because by then I'd be running short of money. I also threw out requests from charities I thought I'd already given to, but it was years before I actually kept a list of my donations and realized how often some of these worthy causes dragged their nets. Such preying on the faulty memories of donors outraged me until I began to get requests which brazenly told me the amount I had already given. I was not being tricked. I was expected to give oftener or anyway more. I mainly gave to organizations for which I could think of no good reason to refuse.

Charities are very vulnerable. We don't forgive them the larceny, mismanagement and bigotry we expect to find in business and government. The Salvation Army hasn't had a nickel in the pot from me since they campaigned in New Zealand against gay rights legislation, and because Amnesty International also ignores the plights of gay prisoners, it gets along without me as well. If I hear one of the organizations for the handicapped is being too paternalistic, I happily strike it off my list.

"I was finally making enough money to give up other work."

When I worked out my first budget for giving, I decided I should use ten percent of my income, an arbitrary figure which comes out of a dim Sunday School past. My only clear memory of that period was being caught by my grandfather in the drugstore where my brother and I were buying cokes with the dime we had been given for the collection plate. Ten percent is arbitrary, too, because my income fluctuates wildly from year to year while my personal wants go up with inflation. Still, one has to begin somewhere.

I also decided I should limit my giving to those organizations which touched some real chord in me. So it was those diseases I was probably in the process of inducing in myself, heart, lung, liver, kidney, I put on my first list as well as those I had or might inherit, arthritis, diabetes, deafness, blindness. Then I added those suffered by other people I'd known. I'd filled a full page before I'd even considered other sorts of good causes, poor children, third world women, illiterates. I hadn't even looked at the stack of pleas for the environment and world peace.

I made a special list of those organizations which, for political reasons, can't offer tax write-offs, like Civil Liberties and Greenpeace. There is a moral purity to that sort of giving that can, in part, balance putting my liquor tax in my budget for giving.

Like a child writing her address from street number and town to The World, The Universe, I tried for categories that began with local issues and gradually expanded to international concerns. Then I might pick one or two in each category for a manageable solution. But is the local garbage dump a charity at all? And how do I choose between lungs and liver? Perhaps I could try alternate years of giving.

I must admit that the list I finally arrived at seemed to me as arbitrary, if not as impulsive, as what I had done without much thought, but at least it was a plan, order made out of chaos.

I do follow it, and I'm never distracted by those fundraisers who now throw in a chance to win a trip to Florida. Aside from the fact that I have no desire to go to Florida, I object to the attempt to confuse my good impulses and right reasons with gambling for holidays. I not only want to know what I'm doing but why I'm doing it.

I am distracted by pleas for organizations made by particular well-known Canadians. Canada is such a small country that I know many of them, and, if Peggy or Ron or Pierre thinks something is worth supporting, it feels almost a personal affront to refuse.

Peculiarly, I'm equally persuaded by the plight of an organization whose government funding has been cut and by organizations for whom the government will provide matching funds.

I do give more than I used to. I sometimes give more than I can afford, never knowing until the end of the year what that ten percent is of. I'm wondering, since I don't really think I'm the only one with such a frail grasp of my charitable behavior, if requests for money shouldn't come with some sort of warning like those on cigarette packages: "For your financial health, don't give more than you can afford." It will probably never be such a problem that we need an organization, Givers Anonymous, for those paying twenty-four percent interest on their impulsive giving, but we do need to be reminded that credit card companies make no distinction between greed and charity. The fundraisers don't remember how many times they've said my name to other fundraisers, nor do they care. But, if I'm not occasionally impulsive, is ten percent of whatever really enough for my part of saving the world?

# SEXUAL LIBERATION IS NOT A SPECTATOR SPORT

{ Undated }

Pornography and erotica are terms like totalitarianism and democracy: they have distinct dictionary meanings, but they are used more often as buzz words in argument about what is good sex and what is bad sex, whether morally or aesthetically, and here their meanings not only blur but drain away. According to the dictionary, pornography is writing about prostitutes, and erotica are representations in pictures or writing which cause sexual feelings or desires. But the dictionary goes on to make it clear that pornography is the more pejorative term by adding such clarifications as "offensive to modesty or decency, lewd, abominable, obscene, disgusting, repulsive." What is erotic is not so heavily weighted with negative judgment, but the term applied to a person means someone "abnormally sensitive to sexual stimulation" or "preoccupied with sex." According to the dictionary, pornography should induce vomiting, erotica somewhat morally suspect sexual desire.

Certainly some of the more violent pornography does make some of us ill, but there would not be the industry there is if the violation of taboos didn't sexually arouse a lot of people. And if it sexually arouses, it is by definition erotic. Conversely, erotic scenes which dwell on romantic settings, love as well as desire between the partners, can be dismissed by the hardier among us as "vanilla sex," not arousing at all and therefore not erotic.

As a writer, in their isolated forms I'm interested in neither, for sexually arousing strangers I will never meet seems a lonely and futile occupation. As for the monetary returns, as with most other writing, they are highly exaggerated. Most of the profits go to the publisher, the printer and the bookseller.

But I am interested in both the pornographic and erotic in relation to people's real behavior as well as the role either plays in their fantasies. For both sexual fantasy and sexual experience reveal a great deal about the people involved, their attitudes toward themselves and other people, their inhibitions and moral natures, their illusions and perceptions. Sexual activity in itself is physically pretty restricted and repetitive, but the meanings given to it by the people involved are complex and ever-changing. If the sexual scenes I write for exploring those meanings happen to be erotic as well, I have to some extent failed, but it would be a mean and arrogant writer who begrudged the loss of a reader's attention to sexual pleasure. Still, my ambition as a writer is to offer insights into the nature of sexual experience rather than masturbatory fantasies. Auden says, "Poetry makes nothing happen." I would like to write that kind of prose.

As a woman I have written endless pages of erotica because I have often been separated from a lover. I therefore associate it as a form with very personal experience, private not in the sense of secret but often limited in meaning for anyone but the intended audience, whose sexual tastes I know, with whom I've shared experience which can, between any two people, eroticize a helicopter, a kitten, a cup of tea, anything that can be associated with sexual memory. A lot of it, not only on the face of it but in fact, is very silly because happy lovers are silly, allowing a playfulness into a relationship which otherwise would give us self-conscious giggles by the time we're ten years old. Both writing it and reading it are also forlorn experiences because it is a pale substitute for real love-making, not an enhancement of it. There is fear in it, too, of the loss absence makes more likely. I hate that song, "When I'm not holding the hand that I long for, I long for the hand I hold." Love letters are also cruel, for calling up desire that can't then be fulfilled causes pain, intensifies loneliness. But even when all other kinds of letters have become obsolete, love letters will still be written by lonely people for lonely people, whether they are separated for hours or months.

An uncle of mine was captain of a destroyer escort during World War II. With so small a number of officers, he had to take his turn at censoring the seamen's letters. Once he simply copied erotic examples from the letters he was reading, put "Dear Mary" at the top of the page, "Love George" at the bottom and sent it to his wife. As was her custom, she gathered her young sons to read out the latest news from their father. Scanning ahead, she blushed violently, crumpled up the letter and threw it into the fire. Had she been alone, her reaction might not have been as violent, and she would have recognized his joke. But it would have been a pornographic rather than an erotic (in the sense of inducing vomiting rather than desire) letter for her because she was not the audience for whom the images were intended.

To write erotica for a general audience, all the longing, silliness, and personal reference must be eliminated. In its place is the careful and graphically detailed description of bodies which must be attractive since they aren't attached to people who are, in themselves, desired. The rituals must also depend on stereotypes of clothing, gesture, speech, not of real love-making between two real lovers who bring themselves and the content of their lives into the experience but of strangers who have no reference to each other but their bodies. They aren't real strangers either who might be apprehensive or clumsy. These are figures in fantasy where the phone never rings, the child never calls, and no one has to go to the bathroom.

Women in the Kensington Ladies' Erotica Society who decided to write and then publish their own sexual fantasies complained that their greatest difficulty was in sustaining the mood for more than a page or two, for the sexual details of a copulation are limited.

Professional writers of erotica (or pornography) solve that problem by introducing a larger cast of characters who can engage in different combinations of sexual acts. They rely also on the use of conventional taboos, fetishes, sadomasochistic behavior in order to prolong the narrative. The need for the bizarre, in relation to most people's real experience, is that arousal is more difficult and harder to sustain in someone who is alone.

Those who defend erotica and pornography as healthy extensions of sexual life argue that the surest pleasure is in masturbation, when one's attention doesn't have to be distracted by other people's desire. Skill at it offers greater autonomy, less danger of forcing unwanted sexual attention on other people. When such writing inspires people to act out some of the fantasies in the text, their sexuality is being liberated from the narrow, puritanical limitations imposed on them by a sexually fearful society, giving them ways to extend sexual attention and sexual interest in circumstances where they might otherwise be bored and indifferent. Sexual fantasy in this argument is value-free and should not be judged as one would judge such actions in "real life."

The difficulty with this argument is that once fantasy is acted out, it is in some sense "real." The actors are not just actors but people in search of sexual gratification. If that involves acts which in real life would humiliate or be humiliating, for instance, then there is a question about how much of a holiday from the self one can take in sexual experience.

Can we afford to indulge in unexamined fantasy with the assurance that it has no effect on our attitudes toward ourselves and other people? I myself think not. Because we live in a sexually fearful society, our fantasies can be infected by that fear, incorporate that negative morality and eroticize both. The desire to punish the body that arouses you is the desire to blame what tempts you. The desire to be helpless and overwhelmed is the desire to abandon responsibility for what you are doing. Acting out such desires reinforces the judgment that sex is wrong, that people who participate in it are either evil or victimized.

It is curious that those who are considered sex's bravest outlaws are dependent on acting out the punishments and shamings in order to enjoy their sexuality. It has to be dangerous, it has to be bad to be good. It mirrors in real life the sexual guilt and abusiveness which have damaged so many people.

Freeing sexual fantasy of its hostile morality and its focus on taboos can't be done by censorship, for that simply reinforces the power of what is taboo. Instead it has to be understood for what it is, a reflection of guilt rather than evil. The Pope and not the pornographer is the source of the problem.

The danger of a code of sexual behavior which brands as evil any sexual act except inside the sanctity of marriage with the purpose of procreation is that it stigmatizes a great range of human behavior with the potential of giving comfort, pleasure, and joy.

Much of what is depicted in pornography is a rebellion against religious teachings and therefore tied to them. If a man's being sexually attracted to a woman weren't considered evil, he would have no desire to punish her for his own feelings. If a man's desire for another man weren't an "unnatural," sinful act, he would have no desire to punish or be punished for it. Sadomasochistic behavior is a morality play that couldn't be staged without the support of religious taboos surrounding sexual desire.

To eroticize punishment is not to be freed from it but to reinforce the connection between desire and guilt, make the one dependent on the other. It is an erotic trap, not a liberation.

The only way sexual fantasy can enhance our sexual lives is for us to create our own, not "value free" but empowering of our own pleasure. Even the least talented of us can do better for ourselves than depend on the mass-produced, impersonal, and necessarily bizarre material that is called either pornography or erotica, which may, as has been claimed, be terms of class distinction only, pornography cheap sleaze, erotica expensively produced and glossy. What is the point of being consumers of sex junk when we are instead at liberty to be imaginative lovers?

Surely there is something very skewed when sexual liberation is offered as a spectator sport or an acting out of someone else's fantasy. Our sexual desire is real. How we express it has consequences in our lives and the lives of our lovers. It can brutalize, frighten, bore, distract, amuse, delight, amaze, transform us, as can any other of our powers. Neither Pope nor pornographer should be allowed to take that responsibility out of our hands.

# FANTASY

{ Undated }

Most dictionary definitions of fantasy are concerned first with distinguishing fantasy from reality: "an unreal mental image," "based on no solid foundation," "a queer notion." Fantasy is downgraded in relationship to the real world, something less than or something false. But when fantasy is considered in relationship to art, the tone of the definitions changes: "a wild, visionary fancy," "an act of the imagination." In this view, fantasy's visionary power can transcend the mundane real world into the realm of truth. The psychological definition of fantasy, "a daydream with some vague continuity fulfilling a psychological need," builds a modest bridge between the seemingly contradictory "false" and "true," for here the unreal is seen to serve a real purpose.

Fantasy is a safety valve, where real emotions can be vented in the imagination instead of allowed to explode in the real world in which they might do damage. Fantasy, in this view, purges the individual, as great art is said to purge society, of otherwise unacceptable emotions. That Aristotelian term "catharsis" has been taken over by psychoanalysis with some modification as "an effective discharge with symptomatic relief but not necessarily a cure for the underlying pathology." Committing murder in fantasy may relieve you of anger at your boss, but it will be an effective safety valve only if you have no real desire to commit murder.

Fantasy based on real desire is rehearsal for action. Murder and grand passion begin there, as do all ambitions. A boy dreaming of himself as a great hero in war is preparing himself to enlist in the army. A girl dreaming of being willing victim to a great lover is preparing herself for the experience. That each of those dreams is among the cultural garbage dumped into their heads makes it all the easier for fantasy to be transformed into fact. The more unreal the content of the fantasy, the harder the fact will be to bear.

Sexual fantasy is commonly used as a safety valve for erotic energy. The content of sexual fantasy indulged in for the purpose of masturbation is astonishingly various. The scene may be a closet empty of everything but a pair of shoes, one glove, or an old sock. A bowl of grapes, a bone, a wounded bird are as capable of arousing individual lust as the memory of an intensely satisfying sexual experience with another person or an elaborately orchestrated orgy.

There are people for whom solitary fantasies are their sole sexual life. For others those fantasies have little relation to their sexual experiences with other people. But for many, sexual fantasy is based on real desire and is the rehearsal for sexual activity in the real world. If fetishes are part of the fantasy, they want partners who understand the erotic value of fetishes. If there is a ritual plot, partners must learn it. Sexual pleasure, if not dependent on these fantasies, is heightened by them.

Is a fantasy so imposed on the real world still a fantasy? Well, if you're supposed to be a nun and I'm supposed to be a novice, sure. If we dress up in costumes, we are not trying to make the roles more real so much as being more elaborate in our make-believe. Sadomasochists stress costume and props as one of the assurances that what they are doing is theatre on its way to orgasmic catharsis rather than any desire to humiliate or harm those real people involved.

The self-conscious acting out of fantasies which link sex with violence or violation of religious taboos is a safety valve only if that behavior is not really desired. Wife beating is not an erotic fantasy being acted out, nor is the raping of nuns or the bashing of queers, but all are common enough practices for us to know the real links between erotic energy and violence.

To keep the barrier between fantasy and reality, we act out scenes as if we were not ourselves, allowing into them all the repressive and punishing images which we are violated by in real life, not transcending taboos but building dependencies on them. Sex, like murder, becomes an unacceptable part of real life, nothing to share with real people, the energy instead "safely" vented in private or shared fantasy where all the accrued guilt and fear can wash around in it, unexamined and unresolved, because none of it is "real."

Fantasy as an activity to keep alive infantile needs, prejudices, fears and anxieties is an abuse of rich raw material which can be used instead to understand ourselves, to integrate our sexual with our social selves.

Fantasy is transformed into art by the aesthetic, moral and intellectual power of the artist. The images and desires of fantasy are understood in their relation to the real world, not in an attempt to keep them isolated. In art as in real life there are consequences for what people do; therefore what they do has meaning.

Being victims of the fantasies guilt and repression have put into our heads is not freedom. Sex as a bad joke is not much progress from sex as evil. Our erotic energy is real. What we do with it has meaning.

# LEGALLY SINGLE

{ March 2001 }

The census taker, a nervously domestic old
man, spread newspapers on our dining room table to avoid mar-
ring it with his jottings. Sitting across from him, I thought of
picking crab or sorting wild huckleberries.

"Head of household?" he began hopefully.

"Helen Sonthoff and I own the house jointly," I answered.

The mortgage broker wondered if perhaps we were the first
women back there in the late '50s to own a house together without a husband or brother to co-sign the mortgage. He had spent
the whole weekend looking through regulations for a reason to
refuse us and hadn't found one.

There was no place on the census form for such joint

ownership. Because Helen was out in the garden, I became head of household.

"Ancestry?" he then asked.

Helen, at her first border crossing into Canada, had said, "American."

"That isn't a category," the immigration official informed her. "Where did your parents come from?"

"The United States."

"Grandparents?"

"The United States."

"Lady, even the people who came over on the Mayflower came from some place else."

"I'm part Indian," Helen said.

The more docile before official questioning, I said to the census taker, "Scottish and German."

He scribbled one word, hesitated, and then said, "You don't have to say German. Scottish is enough."

Still in 1961 it was a rebuke to feel no decent shame.

"Profession?"

"I'm a teacher," I said, still shy of claiming to be a writer, not having published enough to have a right to that title, though I taught only one course at the University of British Columbia and spent the greater part of my time writing fiction.

"Salary?"

"$1,200 a year."

"How many hours a week do you work?"

"It varies. Probably twenty."

"Oh, you teachers are always too modest about the time it takes to prepare classes and mark papers. Let's put down forty."

"Love freely given without conditions."

Though I would have been happy enough to contribute to the knowledge that teachers are grossly underpaid, such exaggeration could hardly be credited.

At this point Helen appeared, puzzled by the newspaper on the table, by the man sitting with me at it.

"Are you going to polish the silver?" she asked.

"You must be the star boarder."

Our relationship survived that census taking.

Now I hear that in the 2001 census taking, I will have the opportunity to declare not only joint ownership of a house but the same-sex nature of my relationship. It's too late for that for me. Helen died last January, and I don't suppose there's a place on the form to be accurate about what sort of widow I am.

The new militants of the gay and lesbian movement are proud of this new opportunity to declare themselves, to have their relationships given the respectability of being officially acknowledged. I expect many more people will fear exposure which could lead to lost custody of children, loss of a job, alienation from church or family. For them it will simply add to the layers of lies they already tell.

How will this new misinformation be used? That we will be grossly under-estimated is certain. We will be perceived by politicians as less of a pressure than we claim we are at ten percent of the population. Those of us who do expose ourselves in the census and tax returns will find ourselves subject to more of the regulations that have plagued heterosexuals for so long, creating false dependencies and arbitrary responsibilities, where before we learned to take real care of each other in creative, communal ways.

A friend of mine told me the other day that he gave a false name to get a Safeway card to ensure that his patterns of purchase couldn't be stored anywhere and sold to anyone to target him as a consumer.

I do like subversive gestures, but, if we are really going to learn to protect ourselves from the quantities of information and misinformation collected in our names, we have to begin to question government's and business' right to know.

Any government policy based on the nature of our sexual relationships is a throwback to a time when women and children were considered property. It is still a cause for nostalgia for those who talk a lot about "family values."

We don't own each other. We are not automatically unequal in a relationship. We've vowed neither to endow each other with all our worldly goods nor to obey. No law should force us into relationships defined by anyone but ourselves. To declare our right to be independent of such control, every adult, regardless of sexual preference or living arrangement, should declare that she or he is legally single, even if, as in my unhappy case, it happens to be true.

# YOU BE NORMAL, OR ELSE...

{ 1991 }

Helen Sonthoff, whom I met in 1954 and with whom I've lived since 1956, has just had a new dental plan offered her in her retirement package. If our relationship were legally sanctioned, I could benefit, too. Since I have spent all my working life either free-lancing or taking temporary positions, I have no retirement plan of any sort except of my own devising. Heterosexual couples often don't even have to be married to enjoy such options. Whenever Helen and I pay our dues, our memberships in the same organizations, we don't pay a couple's rate; we pay two singles. Official invitations now usually say, "and escort," but you can bet the University President doesn't expect two women to show up on one ticket. Whether it's the government or the community or a private corporation, there's usually a bargain for heterosexual couples. But I'm not sure, if you added them all up, any heterosexual couple would think such perks put much of a superior gloss on their lifestyle. If you're the female of the couple, you may want to ask what a little cheap dental work is in comparison to equal pay for equal work, which as a wife you're less apt to be offered, whether you're teaching in a university or typing in an office. And if a man has kids and a wife at home looking after them, talk to him about how far the deductions go in the real cost of keeping his wife at home to raise his children.

What amazes me is that most people really do seem to think that government and business support heterosexuality. If they really did, we'd have decent child care for every child, pay for work done at home, and free education through university. Looking simply at the dollars and cents of it, the government gives us far more encouragement to support charities, cultural institutions, and our favorite political parties than to raise kids. Being heterosexually reproductive is a hugely expensive enterprise of no financial benefit. If the children have financial worth, they and the state rather than the parents benefit.

The material rewards for being heterosexual are minimal. Oh, sure, it would have been nice to have paid leave to go to Helen's mother's funeral, but I couldn't have gone anyway. I had to teach her classes as well as my own. Most private obligations aren't covered in union contracts for anybody. So where do we get the notion that heterosexuality is such a big privilege? It's very simple really, and it's not about rewards at all.

If you're heterosexual, you're normal. I suspect most of us are bisexual and therefore have choices in the ways we arrange to live our sexual lives. If heterosexual really were a biological imperative rather than a social construct, nobody would have to persuade us to pair ourselves off and breed. Some of us might do it anyway, finding tolerable mates and pleasure in children, but I doubt that those would make up the vast, vulnerable majority of us who have been, at one time or another, members of heterosexual unions. Fear of being abnormal and unacceptable coerces people into heterosexual coupledom and parenthood.

That same fear turns us into compulsive consumers. We not only have to be heterosexual, we have to smell heterosexual, have heterosexual skin and hair, own heterosexual appliances and automobiles, live in heterosexual houses, read heterosexual books and go to heterosexual movies. And have heterosexual kids for whom we buy heterosexual toys. It's normal.

As the family becomes a heavier financial burden for men, a more obvious prison of second-rate citizenship for women, the reason for having children less clear all the time, being normal may not be enough to keep people loyal to that choice. Government response to the failure of the family is not to ease financial pressure or offer financial assistance but to increase moral pressure to be normal by limiting the scope of sex education, re-criminalizing abortion, refusing custody of children to lesbians and gay men. "You be normal, or else..."

It's an odd moment for us to want to be legally married, too, for us to demand the right to adopt children, for us to be seduced by "the privilege of heterosexuality" to normalize our own relationships with the state. What we forfeit by these ambitions is our greatest strength: we are free to define our relationships in any way we choose, make our own terms without reference to predetermined roles and expectations.

I don't want to be someone else's wife or husband. I don't want the inequality and dependence built into that heterosexual equation. I don't want to be a deduction or have a deduction. I accept the responsibility of working for my living to take care of my own needs, an important one of which has been time to do my own writing long before it was a source of income. I don't want to answer to anyone else about how I spend either my time or my money, nor do I want anyone to have to answer to me.

I don't want sexual fidelity to be the basis of trust in a relationship. I want to own no body but my own. The loyalty I look for and offer is respect for the autonomy, for the independence of purpose, for the integrity of each of us, love freely given without conditions. Accommodations are gifts, not requirements.

The whole language of heterosexual marriage is set against my view of relationship. "Being of one flesh" is a repellent metaphor for me, a diminishment of two distinct people. "With my body I thee worship." I'm not a worshiper of gods, men or women, but, if I were, my body would be incidental to that practice. The loss of individuality and servitude don't have any place in my sort of love.

Some years ago Helen suggested we should no longer say we didn't believe in the intrinsic value of long-term relationships, the growing length of our own an apparent contradiction to our views. But each of us has had other relationships of shorter duration which we don't count as failures because they didn't last a lifetime. In the heterosexual value system, marriages that end

Jane and Helen in Athens: "gradually money
became less of an all-consuming problem. We could travel."

are defined as failures, however useful, nourishing, lively they might have been along the way.

In a culture that financially punishes parents and dislikes children, it's no wonder the birth rate is diminishing among heterosexuals. The puzzle is why so many more of us are not only bringing children from heterosexual pasts but volunteering to be artificially inseminated or demanding the right to adopt children for our own, then tangling ourselves in the legal confusions of who is actually a parent and who isn't. If children are to survive and thrive among us, we have to be more concerned about loving than owning them, just as we must be among ourselves. Children do not bring meaning to otherwise meaningless lives. They do not satisfy their parents' desire to be normal, nor do they grow up to succeed where their parents failed. Every child must be a wanted child not only by parents but by the neighborhood, the school, the medical service, the whole environment in which that child lives. Too often children are our excuse simply to extend our selfishness to them, make them the cul-de-sacs of our altruism and love. We must learn that they don't belong to us, are not extensions of ourselves. When we really understand that they belong to themselves and the future, our responsibility to all of them is clear, whether we take them as tax deductions or not.

What we must fight for and guard is our right to protect, teach, and heal not only the children but ourselves and each other. What we can teach is "You be normal, or else... you be free."

# THE RIGHT TO BE LEFT

{ September 2005 }

Only a hundred years ago left-handedness was considered a perversity. Left-handed children were discouraged at home and forbidden in school to use their left hands. No matter how clumsy they were at eating, painting, writing, throwing a ball with their right hands, ineptitude was preferred to sinister competence. Even after children often developed stammers as a result of stress, still the restriction persisted. Better for England's King George VI to stammer through his messages to the nation than to eat or sign his name with his left hand. Only in the 1940s did educators and psychologists begin to question the value and count the cost of converting the left-handed. By the 1950s children were free to choose. But in a world designed for the right-handed, left-handed people are by necessity more ambidextrous. As it is for most other minorities in the population, flexibility is a survival skill.

About the same number of people, ten percent of the population, are homosexual, a hundred years ago also considered a sign of perversity, discouraged whenever it was suspected, in cross-dressing, in tastes and attitudes more normal for the opposite sex. But, unlike left-handedness, homosexuality is not so easily identified in childhood and hidden by all but the most obviously masculine women and effeminate men. Even they could and did marry in order to pass as heterosexual. The very ability to conceal may have contributed to both the ignorance of the general population and the harshness of the laws passed against homosexuality. No one was ever banned from work or jailed for being left-handed. The very visibility of their suffering made it easier to understand the plight of the left-handed and come up with remedies for it. Homosexuals were rarely identified except when their behavior was extreme, so they were thought to be only child molesters and gross exhibitionists. The label was not given to those many inept husbands and wives, those lonely bachelors and spinsters, those nuns and priests sheltering in protective covering against the harsh judgment of society, so often internalized.

Until the late 1960s one could still be jailed for five years in Canada for homosexual acts between consenting adults in private. In the 1970s homosexuality was finally removed from the official list of mental diseases.

Today, attitudes toward homosexuality are similar to those toward left-handedness in the 1940s. The pressures on young people to hide and deny their sexuality can have results far more damaging than the identity itself, as the rate of suicide among gay adolescents proved. Schoolyard bullying, once condoned as a useful social pressure to conform, is now generally condemned. In more enlightened schools, lessons in accepting diversity of all kinds are taught. In society at large, openly homosexual people are accepted even in occupations involving the young and frail, and much less often automatically considered security risks.

Now several countries, including Canada, have made marriage legal among gays and lesbians. But homosexuals are not yet seen as a benign minority like those who are left-handed. Both the women's and gay movements, which have been responsible for most of the progress made in the last thirty-five years, still face strong prejudice both culturally and religiously motivated.

The prejudice against the left hand is founded on hygienic principles, the left hand designated for unclean chores, the right for socially positive activities like eating and shaking hands. Access to clean water, soap, and a greater understanding of how germs are transmitted were long established before the left hand was finally liberated.

The prejudice against homosexuality began among the Jews, a beleaguered minority themselves, to protect their religion from the alien beliefs of the Greeks for whom homosexual behavior was associated with religious rituals. Also the Jews needed to protect and increase their numbers and, therefore, insisted that sexual activity be restricted to procreation.

Like so much of Old Testament teaching, prohibitions with at least some useful meaning at the time became articles of faith long after they served any real need. What once may have been unhygienic or a threat to the survival of the tribe must now be seen in more absolute terms as sinister and unnatural. These prohibitions become then not guides to a moral life but tests of blind obedience. Now it is simply not God's will for people to be homosexual.

Because marriage is for so many intimately connected with religious ceremony—even people who are not churchgoers often want to be married in church—the present backlash against homosexual marriage is fierce. For centuries the church's only accommodation of homosexuals has been celibacy, not only in ordinary life but in religious orders and the ministry. The giving up of sexuality characterizes the highest calling to God. Falling short of that ideal, marriage is offered as a way out of sin. "It is better to marry than burn." Even in marriage the only excuse for sexual activity is procreation. How then can homosexuals be allowed blessing for their sexual union?

Just as left-handed people are more ambidextrous than right-handed people, so homosexuals are often more bisexual than heterosexuals, for they grow up in a profoundly heterosexual world, exposed to the pervasive erotica of the culture and all its social pressure to conform. Many are bisexual or even heterosexual in experience in adolescence, often even marry and have children before they declare their real sexual preference.

Children are then brought into homosexual relationships or are conceived in or adopted into them. The desire of some homosexuals to marry is to give such children a greater legitimacy before the law as well as a more defined sense of family and security. Sadly, it is just those quite conservatively oriented people wanting families as much like others as possible who most offend those who would keep them out.

Many more homosexuals have experienced much of what is stifling in family life and have turned away from conventions which have punished them for who they are. They are not as likely to seek acceptance in marriage. They have learned to enjoy the freedom of defining their own relationships and communities to serve the needs they have. Everything from one-night-stands to lifelong partnerships, from nuclear families to communes, the experiments in living go on. Some are messy, self-destructive, others inspired and liberating, but the mistakes have not been imposed and the joys discovered are hard won.

More and more heterosexuals are choosing not to marry, excluding both church and state from defining their relationships, accepting the responsibility for themselves in designing their own privileges and obligations.

Perhaps giving homosexuals the right to marry is a necessary step in teaching heterosexuals that it is a choice, not an obligation. In their new liberation from the necessity of marriage they will be more comfortable with a minority in their midst who have been required for so many years to invent their own lives. No one has to be a child of the church or state but each can be an adult, not bound to ancient customs and prejudices but open to the needs, desires, and requirements of their individual and collective lives.

The only sign of bondage on the otherwise exonerated left hand is the wedding ring. It would be ironic to see that same ring as the ultimate sign of acceptance of homosexuals; most of us would be better off with bells on our toes for the dance of liberation.

# MILLS, 1948-1952

{ 1992 }

When I was a student at Mills, from 1948 to 1952, it was an offense to be sexual, never mind of what orientation. Men were not allowed in our rooms. Even the doors of the smaller living rooms were to be left open if we were entertaining men. When President White discovered that his eight-year-old son sometimes dropped by to sail paper boats in my sink, the boy was ordered to stay out of the dormitories.

Homosexuality was never mentioned, even by the visiting woman doctor enlisted especially to give us two lectures on sex, about which she confessed she was very embarrassed. Mainly she was there to inspire us to keep our virginity as our most precious gift to our husbands. Then we were asked to write a paper entitled, "A Livable Sex Philosophy."

My instructor invited the Dean of Women to attend a conference with me about the essay I handed in.

The Dean said to the instructor, "This essay is intended to be funny."

"Is this meant as a joke?" the instructor demanded.

"I thought having them all the same would get dull," I admitted.

I don't remember now what I wrote, except for the last line which was, "I prefer to remain flexible." I certainly hadn't declared myself a lesbian, but I had refused to write the party line.

Homosexuality was never mentioned in any of my literature classes either though we studied, at the instigation of a closeted but restless gay teacher, Christopher Isherwood's *Prater Violet*, in which he uses letters of the alphabet rather than names for lovers in order to conceal their gender.

We didn't discuss homosexuality when we studied Shakespeare's sonnets. But we didn't discuss anti-Semitism when we studied *The Merchant of Venice* either, though there was in that class a survivor of the holocaust. Nor did we discuss the rampant misogyny in much that we read.

Ignoring issues that were basically, personally important to us was presented as a scholarly discipline, a training in objectivity. Literature concerned aesthetics. I learned a lot that has been useful to me all my life about conceits and metaphors, metrics and sentence structure, plot and subplot lines. If I learned anything else from literature, I kept it to myself in superior scholarly silence.

As the substance of literature seemed to be nobody's business, so our own substance was nobody's business either as long as we kept silent about it. Our teachers didn't have to cope with our messy complexities, and, as long as we didn't either, we got on swimmingly. Remembering who we were and what we represented had to do with being polite, well-behaved and properly dressed for whatever occasion.

When one young woman raced through the dorm corridors, dodging in and out of various sleeping porches shouting, "I am not a virgin," in high good spirits, she was thought to be joking, too, for those who heard her. The really polite didn't listen.

Tolerance in those days was mainly negative virtue, the learning what not to say, what might offend, rather than attempting to understand and include the differences among ourselves. In a way, to be ignored is better than to be mocked and castigated. Fewer people rebel in such a climate. More people crack under the strain.

We didn't know enough, any of us, to believe we could change an atmosphere dangerous to our health and sanity. I was afraid and ashamed of my fear, afraid not only of my college friends, my good and concerned teachers, but also of my family, of the whole silent, ignorant, bigoted world I lived in which could, if I broke my silence, discredit and banish me.

I was in Europe for most of the McCarthy homosexual witch hunts in the early '50s, but I date the beginning of liberation from that incredible display of internalized homophobia. Jessamyn West said to me, "He should be tried as a homosexual himself." "That tactic would be as bad as his own," I answered. "It would be poetic justice," she insisted. Back to aesthetics again.

"When I was a student at Mills, from
1948 to 1952, it was an offense to be sexual,
never mind of what orientation."

But at least the silence had been broken, and, if the climate for homosexuals in the United States was worse than it had ever been, the brutal hypocrisy and injustice shocked some people into new insights, planted the seeds of rebellions which would flower in the '60s and '70s.

With no such insight into the future, I left the United States for good in 1956 and have lived in Canada ever since, where among a more modest and tentative people I have found it easier to take responsibility for who I am and whom I love.

When my first novel, *Desert of the Heart*, was published in 1964, some people accused me of being a discredit to my family, to Mills, to the university where I then taught, but I was not disowned, nor did I lose my job. A great many people then and over the years have thanked me for writing affirmatively about love between women.

Being in those years the only publicly acknowledged lesbian in Canada distorted perceptions of me as a writer but also gave me an opportunity to address prejudice against homosexuality before national audiences. To this day, when I'm being interviewed ostensibly because I am a writer but really because I am a lesbian, I use such occasions to educate people whose basic bigotry is often simple ignorance.

Because of my notoriety, I was reluctant at first to be associated with the women's movement, not wanting the cause that should matter to all women to be discredited by my membership. Only when undeclared lesbians in the movement began to be challenged and removed did I realize that invisibility would cause greater harm than our frank presence.

I have worked in the women's movement, the gay movement, worked for a coalition politics joining together all those minorities which finally make up the vast majority of people disenfranchised by governments who have not yet been made to serve the needs and defend the rights of all people.

In 1973, I finally reluctantly accepted a commission from Doubleday to write *Lesbian Images*. I hadn't enough time to write fiction, and I was tired of the limiting label. My research for the chapters on religion and psychiatry angered me enough to give me energy to write the book, for in both fields the history of abuse of homosexuals is appalling.

I went on to examine specific writers who had dealt with lesbian identity and experience in fiction, biography and autobiography, for in such works there is far more insight than in religious debate or pseudo-scientific argument. I couldn't ignore that bad old chestnut *The Well of Loneliness*, but I could point out that Virginia Woolf's *Orlando*, that long love letter to Vita Sackville-West, was published without moral uproar in the same year. Discussing Willa Cather, Ivy Compton-Burnett, Elizabeth Bowen, Colette, Violette Leduc, and May Sarton, I could argue that lesbian sensibility was far from marginal for many of our best women writers.

*Lesbian Images* is not about aesthetics. In my frankly subjective approach to the substance of the books I considered, I was breaking the scholarly rules I'd been taught, but in those years scholarly attitudes were changing, too. Women's Studies courses had begun to be offered as well as ethnic studies of various sorts.

While I was working on *Lesbian Images*, the American Psychiatric Association took homosexuality off its list of mental disorders, and religious debate began in many churches where it still goes on with increasing candor if not moral insight.

In 1983, I was called to New York City by the Fund for Human Dignity, a national organization for raising money for homosexual causes, to attend a banquet at the Plaza Hotel. Mario Cuomo, the Governor of New York, was a guest speaker. I received an award of merit for my "contribution to the education of the American public about the lives of lesbians and gay men." As I stood to accept the award, I was aware that I felt none of the stage fright I was accustomed to even after years of public speaking. There among hundreds of strangers I was, nevertheless, one of them, not a single example of a reviled minority trying to win over a hostile or indifferent audience.

There is much more acceptance and much greater freedom for homosexuals now than there was in 1952 when I graduated from Mills, both at Mills and in the country. But immigration officials can still stop me at the border and refuse me entry because of my sexual orientation. Congress still tolerates people like Jesse Helms, whose homophobia allows him to refuse federal aid for educating gay kids about AIDS. We are still being drummed out of the military, and we aren't welcome in the Scouting movement. The head of the National Endowment for the Arts has been fired for giving grants to homosexual artists. Laws to protect us from discrimination are slow to be passed and still too easily rescinded.

Politics is like housekeeping. If we are to live in a healthy environment, we have to keep cleaning it up. We have learned that tolerance isn't a conspiracy of silence on topics about which we might have different views. But, if we are to live in a world in which true courtesy is understanding and accepting differences, we have to practice that courtesy every day. We have to speak.

# IN THE VALLEY OF THE SHADOW

{ January 2007 }

Working for a living was Adam's curse as bearing children was Eve's. The sentence they shared was death. They were punished for their appetite for the knowledge of good and evil. They gave up innocence. They grew up. I find it hard to imagine that without that apple there wouldn't be work, sex and death. Maybe we just wouldn't know ahead of time that foraged food runs out, that sex produces offspring, that everything sexed dies. So the curse really is a foreknowledge of what anybody would rather not know. The bad flaw in the story is the suggestion that, if we didn't know, it wouldn't happen.

Why else would we cherish and protect the young and blame them for their appetite for the apple, whether for paper route, masturbation, or a curiosity at funerals?

We work, copulate and die. There it is, and if it's not God's fault it has to be our own. Why blame anyone? It's the apple's fault for giving us a taste for judgment.

There's really nothing the matter with work. We all have been known to enjoy it, even to indulge an obsession for it. Workaholism is surely more common than an addiction to alcohol, drugs, gambling or video games. And therefore there is something wrong with it. It is supposed to be a judgment, a punishment, the way outside the garden we learn money doesn't grow on trees. There's no free lunch working your way to the grave. It's called working for a living, and we're supposed to be no more than resigned to it.

There's nothing really the matter with sex either. We might enjoy it as much as our appetites suggest if we weren't constantly threatened with the consequences not only of conception or disease but death itself, since mortality is a consequence of our sexuality. Otherwise, like simpler life forms, we could divide ourselves to multiply and return death to accident rather than inevitability. We are like all those spawning fish going up the river to die, only we know it. A common metaphor for orgasm is death. The pleasures of our bodies betray us.

There is something the matter with death. The poet e.e.cummings, using his idiosyncratic punctuation, wrote:

dying is fine) but Death

?o
baby
i

wouldn't like

Death if Death
were
good:

Being conceived, being born is winning a lottery against
enormous odds, the waste of sperm and eggs a lavish extravagance beyond imagining. To be allowed such hardly credible
luck only to know the price is death is to be locked into a dead-
end fairytale, no prince to kiss the princess, no princess to kiss
the frog. Birth is the kiss of death.

Why did Adam and Eve choose to know? The serpent didn't
force; he tempted. If the apple is mortal food, we cannot live
without it. Even beyond the grave, if we imagine it, we conceive
justice, not mercy. It's the way we forgive God our lost innocence
as we don't seem to be able to forgive ourselves.

The tacked-on part of the story about God's finally forgiving us is neither just nor merciful. He had to beget and kill his
only son to do it, setting an example of such outrageous child
abuse one could wish he hadn't loved the world as much as that.
Sacrificing the innocent to redeem the guilty makes murderers
by proxy of us all, gold stars in our windows for the sons we've
given, the sons we've lost for the promise of our own salvation.
It's not just a bad bargain; it's no real bargain at all.

We claim guilt to reduce death to something of our own choosing out of which we may escape through our own or others' efforts. To have no choice, to have no escape, to know that we don't, is the defining knowledge of our lives.

In the valley of the shadow of death, the choice is not between innocence and guilt but between ignorance and insight. Our work is to seed the earth with flowers, poems and children, not to transcend death but to leave an earth worth inheriting for the gifts of life to come.

"In singular old age I sit in the chair of a grandmother and wear her rings, surrounded by walls raised by my father. I have the Indian baskets which once belonged to my great-grandmother."

# A LAW UNTO HIMSELF

{ March 2007 }

I did not like my grandmother's doctor, and I didn't understand why she did. He was a tall, arrogant, ugly man who assumed he was attractive to all females, not because he bothered to charm them but simply because he offered them his random, condescending attention. Grandmother was charmed. She had half a dozen chronic ailments, any one of which might require hospitalization. He so overcharged her for his many house and hospital calls, she claimed to have built one wing of the local hospital. He told her she subsidized his work with the poor. She also inadvertently overfed his large dog, who often stole steaks or a roast from the kitchen counter, to the dismay of the cook and the disappointment of dinner guests.

I did not have much to do with him until the summer I moved in with my grandparents after my grandfather had had a stroke and was bedridden. I was only fourteen, but it was during the war and no nurses were available. The doctor came in once a week to check on both old people. He gave no instructions. He cast no more than an appraising sexual eye on me. Once I tried to confide in him that I was frightened I wouldn't know what to do in an emergency. He said dismissively, "Death isn't an emergency."

Years into her widowhood my grandmother said she didn't mind all her physical handicaps, but she would really hate to lose her mind. In the last year of her life, she did, had lurid sexual fantasies about her aging nurses' imagined lovers, became rowdy and unreasonable until the help quit, and my parents moved in with her to cope.

Her doctor had begun to raise money to build a retirement home for people like my grandmother, with plenty of money but without the ability any longer to run an establishment of her own. He tried to persuade her to invest in it, but she was beyond such considerations by then.

Restless, bewildered, longing to be allowed to go home, which was for her the home of her childhood, she went nights without sleep. My mother, trying to comfort and quiet her, sat through one whole night singing with her, Grandmother still remembering the words of popular songs of the last seventy years.

The next morning, when she finally slept, the doctor came. "I've kept her alive to see her grandchildren grown, her first great-grandchild born," he said. "It's enough."

He gave her a shot and told my parents not to try to rouse her. Hours later she died in that sleep.

The doctor saw his elegant senior citizens' residence built, the first of many that followed. In time my parents moved there to be sure they wouldn't burden their children with the infirmities of their old age. Every time I visited them there, I had to pass a portrait of the doctor hanging in the front hall, dead now in his turn. I found myself wondering if one of his several doctor children had taken the responsibility of his death as he had probably taken the responsibility of many others.

Arrogant men like him are not as free now to play god with their patients. Such doctors can be charged and tried as criminals. I have heard some doctors complain that those who lobby for assisted suicide have cast too much light on the suffering of the dying and taken the right of mercy killing out of doctors' hands where it should belong, outside the law since so many of the dying, like my grandmother, are beyond choice. The doctor's decision, in the face of great distress and suffering, may be, in order to do no more harm, to end a life.

My mother, after my father's stroke and heart attack, could ask to have life support discontinued. "I promised him I wouldn't let him be a vegetable." Though she would have liked to shorten her own dying, she could only starve herself against her cancer because there was no one with the knowledge or courage to help her die. My grandmother's doctor would have.

That ugly, arrogant man, a law unto himself, fleeced the rich, served the poor, built an elegant retirement home for the comfort and dignity of the old, and kept alive and killed as he saw fit. I did not like the man. But I have never forgotten what he so long ago, and I thought callously, told me, "Death is not an emergency."

# LEAVE-TAKING

{ 1984 }

Moving around so much for the first twenty-
five years of my life taught me to leave places lightly. Only when
I was old enough to fall in love did places become linked with
people and therefore invested with personal meaning for me.
A particular street corner, the curve of a river might, even when
it had been long deserted, resonate with lost joy. I can still weep
at films of London streets or the sweep of the Sussex Downs,
particularly in B movies, but the experience of actually returning
to that city or countryside has always been too rich in the present
for there to be much room for nostalgia. "On this bridge," I
can begin to think, but, if I'm not immediately distracted by
the passing scene, I am as soon caught up in Helen's reactions,

for she is both there with me and my companion of thirty years.

Still, I wondered when we planned a trip to New England last fall to Concord, Massachusetts, where we met and taught for two years, and to Lyme, New Hampshire, where Helen's mother had owned a farm, scene of family Christmases those years ago, and of a final summer, two years after she died, when we had to pack the place up and sell it. We hadn't been back for twenty years. Did I suggest my parents go with us partly as a way to keep the present sharply in focus? I did know, if there were to be nostalgia, Helen and I wouldn't share it as a common source. For Helen the eastern landscape is far richer in her past life and family than it is for me.

What we could all share was the purpose for going: the autumn color. Even the best photographs can't catch it, for, though they show the whole landscape aflame in every color from the golds of birch, ash, elm, and aspen through oranges and pinks to the dark red of dogwood and red maple, they cannot provide the sharp clarity of air, scented with smoke and ripe apples, or show the drift and dance of leaves, or tempt the ear with the sound every child loves, the scrunch and scrabble of leaves underfoot, as loud as kicking at paper bags and yet sharp and fragile because one treads on the skeletons of leaves. After the humid heat of summer, the erupting lushness of that short season, the cool harvest air can also taste of the coming of snow. There is urgent, new energy to bring the crops in quickly, but it's crazed energy, too, in the flare of all that fragile dying. The pumpkins in the fields glow even in the dusk, and so do the apples on the already leafless trees.

I haven't remembered this from thirty years ago as the constant intoxication it is for me now. I can't imagine how anyone stays indoors, gets on with the job, why the whole village isn't out of doors at least, twirling and staggering into piles of leaves. Oh, there is an occasional berserk child but the rest of Lyme, New Hampshire, goes on with its business, whether running the inn or the store, whether getting the church ready for a wedding or baking bread or milking the cows.

I do remember that industry, but they are mostly winter scenes in deep snow, the endless emergencies of furnaces going wrong in the chicken houses, of young stock free and headed to Hanover on the main road, none of which prevented people from getting to church, getting the Christmas dinner on or even sometimes reading by the fire in the book room, whose windows still had thick pine shutters to pull against raiding Indians.

And I remember summer, the heat, the relief of sudden storms, the dismantling of that beautiful old house, room by room, finding stashes of things undisturbed for the twenty-five years Helen's mother had lived there with her friend Florence, bottled fruits and vegetables in the cellar dating back to the war.

In autumn, I must have been at Concord, getting on with my teaching job. I do remember there the fields of pumpkins I saw from a train window on my way to Helen's house in Littleton, but I wouldn't have said my intoxication then had anything to do with the season.

How long has it been since I've been old enough to let the weather in, or in again, as I must have when I was a child? And how long have I been old enough to return to such a place with no one left alive to call on? We do go to the cemetery to find

Helen's mother's grave, all four of us, my parents a little shy of what that might mean to Helen, if not to me. I have never spoken extravagantly of my love for parents other than my own, and I was raised by a woman who denies only one emotion: grief. I had not been there to bury Ruth, and Helen, concerned so much for the living as one is at such a time, siblings, aging aunts, Florence, can't remember quite where the grave is. My mother is nervous to find it for her, stalks the rows of headstones without distraction because she does not recognize the number of names Helen and I do, the neighbors, the friends who belong to those long-ago Christmases, even to the final auction when the farm was sold. My father detaches himself more easily, goes to take a picture of a young sugar maple, in full blaze, and it is under that tree we find Ruth's grave. Florence must have planted it there. Mother wants it to be a simple joy. Dad would like it to be his present, the finding and photographing. For Helen and me the complexities needn't be shared. Florence is not buried here. She must have been taken off by her sister, buried with relatives in Rochester, but her tree is here.

We all also go to the farm, down past the house we had renovated for Florence after Ruth died, past the chicken "prisons" as the family called them, past the barn next to the house, painted red now instead of white, a utility room added along the kitchen and dining room wall. We sold the place to a New York lawyer, the only one in those days with the money to buy it, $35,000 for an early settler's house, modernized and extended but itself at the core, for forty-some acres and outbuildings. Four years ago a young family bought it for $235,000. They are in love with it, want to know every moment of its history back to its beginnings.

Helen's family at her mother's farm, Lyme, New Hampshire.

The young wife welcomes us, asks us in. The living room seems smaller somehow, though there are the two-foot-wide pine boards, the old beams, and there are the words Ruth had carved over the fireplace, "Grow old along with me. The best is yet to be." The book room is as lived in as it was in the days we knew it. Helen will go back a couple of days later to talk about what she knows of the history of the house, a duty for her. I needn't go back, put my mind not to remembering but to worrying about that young family saddled with a killing mortgage. Obviously there is money in their families, but of the sort to provide expensive cars and holidays when they haven't operating money to keep the place warm in winter. But I suspect it has always been a struggle to live there, nearly a given in the harsh New Hampshire winters.

*Leave-Taking* 173

While Helen is away at the farm, I tend my mother who has come down with a heavy cold, and nearly absent-mindedly I read the mood of the inn, where this morning we were given continental breakfast instead of the large country breakfast offered in the last few days. I assume it may simply be Sunday, which the owners take off, the woman not at the desk with her friendly banter, the man not cooking breakfast or tending the bar.

The soups offered for dinner are too rich for an invalid's palate. The attentive substitute at the desk suggests we cross the green to the store and pick up a can of chicken soup which can be heated in the kitchen and a tray provided for Dad to take up to Mother before we have our own dinner. Helen, just back, volunteers to go, perhaps needing to stride out into quiet after her social afternoon.

We contemplate lobster for our own dinner. Helen hesitates and then is persuaded by Dad's enthusiasm. He is more talkative than usual at dinner, trying to make up for Mother's absence. Whenever we are all together, each of us has natural responsibilities, and Mother's is keeping us all amused.

At the end of the meal, just as I reach down for my handbag, Helen tips sideways from her chair. For a second, I think she has somehow simply lost her balance, but she is lying on her side, unconscious, a gash by her left eye made by her glasses, lying twisted and bloody beside her.

I am on my knees, trying to turn her oddly rigid body, trying to loosen the bow at her throat. A woman from another table in the dining room who is a nurse is down with us on the floor, taking Helen's pulse. She rouses but doesn't focus.

"Take deep breaths," the nurse instructs.

"What is it?" Helen asks, and I see her take in my face.

"You fainted," my father says, standing behind me.

She gags and swallows.

"I'm going to be sick."

"Take deep breaths."

I see her distress and embarrassment.

"Shall we help you to the bathroom?"

My father gets behind her and lifts her to her feet. The nurse and I on either side of her walk her toward the bathroom, but in the doorway of the hall she loses consciousness again, and I have to let her down gently against me to the floor, vomit flowing out of the side of her mouth into her hair, onto the floor.

Helen is conscious again, apologetic and bewildered. I clean the vomit from her hair with my hand, and Dad has found paper towels to clean up the floor. The woman on the desk has called the emergency crew. We've been able to move Helen to a couch by the time they arrive. They are giving her oxygen. They want to take her immediately to the hospital in Hanover, ten miles away. I am asked to get any medicine she's been taking. On the way back downstairs, I have only a moment to tell my mother what has happened, where we are going.

"I'll follow you," Dad says as I climb into the ambulance behind the stretcher.

As the ambulance swings out into the road, I feel the sour weight of my own undigested dinner and wonder if Helen will be made sick again, but she seems alright, answering questions the attendant puts to her not only for information but to check her alertness. I hear in those questions concern for stroke, heart attack, diabetic attack. The attendant turns from Helen to radio instructions to the hospital. I can look out the back door of the ambulance and see my father at the wheel of our rented car, and I know his own nervous system is behaving just as mine does, in abeyance to will.

He has somehow parked the car and got to us before we go through the emergency entrance doors. When I am asked to provide information about insurance, he stays with Helen, holding her hand, smiling at her, and the attendants don't order him away, perhaps assuming he is her husband.

I have had enough experience in hospitals as "not next of kin" to be agreeable but assertive.

"I am next of kin," I say firmly.

"Relationship?"

"We've lived together for thirty years."

"The gentleman?"

"He's my father."

I have also had enough experience with emergency wards to be very impressed by this one, the efficiency and kindness of everyone dealing with us. We know the tests which are to be administered and why. We know how long they will take. We even know there is a possibility that Helen can be released when they're over.

Both my father and I need to clean up. The sour smell on my hands isn't offensive to me. It smells of Helen's life, and it is not the first time I've had its primitive reassurance.

We sit in the waiting room, neither of us talkative, but Dad again takes on Mother's role, as far as he can.

"Her color's good," he says. "At first I was frightened—a stroke or a heart attack—but I think she's going to be fine."

176

I haven't had time to be frightened, and I am nearly sure now that nothing serious is wrong, but I am glad of all the tests.

This is the hospital where, twenty-two years ago, Ruth died of kidney failure. Helen arrived in time to have her mother reach out, take her hand and say, "I'm taking this one with me," before she slipped into a final coma.

The tests are all negative. The doctor comes in to explain that it has been simply a temporary overloading of the nervous system, a tiring day perhaps? (I cannot know) a rich dinner, an attempt to stand up. It's unlikely to happen again. She needs only to rest for a day.

We're back at the inn just before ten o'clock. The kind woman at the desk says she planned to check on Mother herself if we weren't back soon. "Thank you so much," I say.

"You're the one," she answers sympathetically. "I'm glad you're here to take care of them."

It is a remark Helen overhears on her way up the stairs.

"My poor darling, traveling with such a bunch of old crocks."

Dad lost a tooth just before we left, and we had to get him emergency dentistry.

I won't feel daunted. Hard jokes is all they are being, Dad's tooth, Mother's cold, Helen's fainting. I just don't want to be next.

It is Mother for whom the evening has been the most trying, lying there helpless to do anything but imagine the worst.

"You really must learn to drive again," she says to me, and I know she's buried Helen beside her mother and sent me home alone, incapable of caring for myself on our little island where there is no public transport.

I don't resent it. The interdependence and therefore self-sufficiency of any long-devoted pair prompts other people to the bleakest images in an emergency.

I've put my mother or my father under the sod more than once, a useless rehearsal of my own helplessness because my parents have never needed anything more than my easy love, and what would it be worth to either of them without the other? Something surely, but shamingly inadequate.

Mother and Helen rest on Monday. Dad goes out for solitary picture-taking. I go down to the parlor to take notes on the local trees, to read. Still the owners of the inn are not in evidence. We've had another continental breakfast, served by a young waitress in a sullen daze. The woman on duty for such a long day yesterday is here again today, looking strained and tired.

"Isn't it time you had a break?" I ask.

"Yes," she says. "I'm sorry about breakfast this morning. It isn't usually like this."

I wait.

"The owners' youngest son was killed in a car accident late Saturday night."

I had seen him on Saturday night at the desk talking to his mother, leaning over her with an unlit cigarette dangling from his mouth, a slight, tense boy of perhaps twenty.

"Since when do cigarettes cost $5?" she was asking, her tone light.

"I want a couple of beers. It's Saturday night."

I wondered what a twenty-year-old was doing bullying small sums of money from his mother, surly with her in front of guests.

"He seemed an unhappy kid," I say.

She nods. "Over the last few months...."

"It's a very hard age."

"Like my own boy. His father died when he was sixteen. Oh, he's all right now, quiet... sometimes too quiet. They were friends."

She needs to talk to someone not involved, where her own shocked feelings won't compete with more important griefs. She's had only a few hours' sleep in the last thirty-six. The boy was alone. The people in the other car were hurt, but they survived. He died soon after he got to the hospital. The two older sons are coming home. There will be a graveside service tomorrow.

"The minister?"

"Oh, he's alright now that's he's had some trouble of his own...."

When I knew Lyme, the woman minister shared the rectory with a woman doctor who some time later killed herself, after they'd moved away.

A young couple come in to register. He pauses on the way up the stairs and asks, "Dress code?"

"Casual," the woman at the desk replies.

The phone rings. She answers, listens, says, "As well as can be expected. They got a little sleep last night."

Helen comes down the stairs in her coat. I put on my jacket and we walk across the green past the church to the store to find food for lunch we'll eat in our rooms. I tell her what has happened. On the counter there is a collection box for the dead boy. Helen puts money into it.

We will be gone, on our way to see old friends of my parents in Vermont, by the time he is buried tomorrow afternoon, too young to have learned to let the weather in, too young to have gone back to a place where everyone he's known lies in the graveyard, beneath the flaming trees.

I don't grieve for him. I grieve for his parents for whom he must now stay an unfinished spirit beyond their reach to help.

My mother would think it none of our business to take any part of that sorrow as our own. Enough to carry our own difficulties cheerfully into whatever is before us in Vermont, in Massachusetts: old friends, godchildren, nephews, lit by the light of the dying year.

But for me the present sucks up memory, the dead, love, grief, as gusts of wind suck up the leaves. I haven't any longer the heart for light leave-taking. I think perhaps Helen never has.

# THERE ARE LEFT THE MOUNTAINS

{ 2004 }

Back in the '60s when my private work, ten long apprentice years of it, began to attract some public attention, I was startled to be paid a thousand dollars for a novel two years in the making and also a thousand dollars for a short-short story I had written in one afternoon. It was an importantly freeing experience. It taught me that the world's values and my own were so out of kilter I could never measure myself in the world's terms. Years later when a university archives paid me far more for my wastepaper than I'd ever been paid for published work, I felt the same larky freedom along with gratitude that the mad world, like a slot machine or lottery, occasionally paid off in my favor.

Why then do I feel a rush of moral indignation when friends

are so ill- or arbitrarily served? In the late '60s, one year half a dozen people I knew, after years of applying, suddenly received Canada Council grants. Why now, I wondered. A friend replied, "Because they don't any longer really need them." At my age, it is now not so often the balance of neglect and lunatic honors as it is the public obituary moments, the last rites, at which I flame out of private grief into outrage.

Last week Toni Onley's death was announced on the radio just as I was waking and elaborated on that night toward the end of the late TV news. I watched, waiting in vain for a glimpse of one of his paintings. In one shot, Toni was on a Vancouver beach threatening to burn his paintings in protest against unfair taxation. Only the corners of a couple of frames were visible. Most of the footage was of a stretch of river where his small plane went down, the wires across the river which might have contributed to the accident. Then much older footage showed his small plane wedged into the fissure in a glacier like a pencil into a pencil sharpener, and there was Toni, unshaven, lying in a hospital bed talking about that long-ago accident. It gave him even more publicity than his threatened picture-burning on the beach, certainly more than any of his numerous shows. There was not one image of any of his great accomplishments as an artist recording his own visions of the great unpopulated wildernesses of this country.

Well, he was a showman, I think to myself, and remember a day here on Galiano when I was being interviewed by an urban journalist who couldn't imagine what there could be to write about out of life on this little, out-of-the-way island. The sound of a plane momentarily distracted us. Half an hour later Toni was at the door, his boots full of water from having waded ashore from his small seaplane, wanting his socks dried, very pleased with himself for having found me simply on a sociable whim.

I have owned only one Onley. I gave it to a friend some years ago where I could still call on it quite regularly until I could no longer visit friends. I can see it still, don't really need my memory refreshed for that particular configuration of mountain, sea and sky, its characteristic grays, blues and whites. I have often seen Toni's vision in the landscapes I've passed through, his light, his mists, his rocky profiles. Toni Onley, along with Tak Tanabe, John Koerner, Jack Shadbolt, and Gordon Smith, taught me to see this world as I would never have on my own. For years I have lived in their British Columbia, on my walls, in public galleries, in reproductions as well as in the place itself.

For those familiar and dear to us, physical memory is a part of grief. We want to and do remember Toni's bantam energy, his rapid tenor voice, the eager bluff of his needs. And, of course, we remember the spectacular public displays—he, after all, did force a change in the tax laws—and embarrassments, surviving that expensive night on a glacier, pictures of which his photographer companion could not later sell to an in-flight magazine. Instead, he and Toni were expected for weeks at a time to give away interviews about that harrowing night.

Eventually, however, Toni Onley will be remembered as he should be for his paintings, the serene or menacing silences of them, light-struck or shadow-darkened, innocent of or indifferent to the transient self-importance of human beings. So the poet Robinson Jeffers is remembered for his words:

> when the cities lie at the monster's feet there
> are left the mountains.

# GRIEF

{ 2001 }

$W$hen I was young, I had fears about committing myself to a relationship. The first was that I would cut myself off from infinite possibilities. With more experience, I feared that no woman would be willing to take a relationship with me seriously against the demands of a man or any family member who laid firmer claims on her loyalty. Then finally I was afraid that commitment would leave me vulnerable to loss of a sort I couldn't endure.

After I had shared forty-five years of living with Helen Sonthoff, she died. The door of life slammed in my face. People writing letters of condolence spoke about dreaming of Helen. She didn't appear in my dreams for months, and, when she did briefly, she was distressed and damaged, out of reach of my care. I was confronted with what I had exactly dreaded, a grief stupid and numbing. I slept badly and briefly, found eating pointless, and felt appalled that I had no way to access forty-five years of good living for any kind of comfort. It was a grief that felt almost a betrayal of the deep joy of my life.

And yet, at the hardest and loneliest hours, I did know that it was a small price for what I might have, as a self-protective youngster, avoided. "The last gift you gave her," a friend wrote, "was to outlive her."

Learning how to survive is, at first, simply a series of distractions which begin with a love/hate relationship with everything Helen loved, from daffodils to children's laughter, from Christmas to lima beans.

I don't now try to make sense of that loss. I learn to make use of it instead. The house I prepared for Helen's broken hip, to which she never returned, now shelters a friend badly hurt in a car accident, a friend about whom Helen used to say, "Just seeing her face makes me feel better." It does me, too.

"Remember," an old friend wrote to me as she was dying, "Love is forever." Risk, grow, grieve. Helen's like will not walk this earth again, nor I love like that again, but the care I learned is useful still for all she and I learned to love together.

# LOVE'S ONLY RIVAL

(December 2005)

Death is the only real rival of love. No important relationship ends except in death. Even the loves of childhood, left long ago, are still lively not only in memory but in imagination. That manic little boy with a hundred silly faces may have grown up to be a stand-up comic or a college professor, but, as long as he is out there in the world somewhere, he is mine to wish well. My nearly twin cousin Frank, however, with whom I shared the burden of an older brother, the humiliation of being left at home, too young for swimming-meet or circus, died in a plane crash just before we turned forty, deserting forever the power of my care. In my own fashion I can pray for the living but not for the dead. For me whatever the soul is is

186

incarnate in the flesh, and, deprived of that sweet body, I may be able to remember love but not go on living in its hope. Possibility turns into the dust of regret. "What if…" becomes "If only…."

"Grief is self pity," my mother said. "Get over it."

That dictum seems useful for all lively losses because it is very difficult to wish another well when I'm feeling sorry for myself. Most broken promises should never have been made. Most assumptions are false. Beyond disappointment, beyond need, there is a remarkable freedom to care, without self-reference, for another, to be glad he or she is out there contributing to the world that uniqueness of being each of us is.

For the dead, however, I see no way past grief. No, of course, it's not for them. No matter what relief there may be in death, which spares people as much pain as it does pleasure, it stops off the power of love, for which the dead have no need. The only place for love to go is back into the past, not to relive it—one can't—but to make amends for every missed opportunity, failure of imagination, a futile exercise which only breaks the heart over and over again.

What's wrong with love itself is the lover wanting to be too good to be true. One can be in emergencies, when all the sweet pettiness and silliness of life fall away and stoic heroism is easy. While we live in love, we don't much mind its daily failures, absent-mindedness, self-absorption, fatigue, because there is time, lovely lengths of it, to compensate. And we do, periodically, joyfully, serve love well. It is relatively easy to forgive ourselves the lapses when there is all the time in the world to be better. Or at least good enough.

Guilt and fury are as much a part of grief as sorrow. We want to be absolved of another's death, however innocent of it we appear in the world's eyes to be. Because we can't be, we rage against the dead, who are as safe from our anger as from our love. "Why couldn't you have run away to sea, fallen in love with someone else, taken holy vows?" Death in most circumstances is not a choice, which makes it all the harder to accept. And it is final. No one can be wooed, bribed, ordered away from it.

Grief is, it sometimes seems to me, as absolute. We wear ourselves out in it, but few of us die of it. We learn instead to live around its edges, even take short holidays from it, but distractions are temporary. At its quietest it is a heavy, silent emptiness, a central blind spot without light or shadow. If we dare to love again, we are cautious and reluctant, not because we are afraid we might not survive another loss but because we are afraid we might.

# I WANT TO SPEAK ILL OF
# THE DEAD

{ July 1997 }

I first understood how competitive grief can be sitting with my grandmother and her sister-in-law who were discussing the hats they would wear to my grandfather's funeral before he had died. Spinster Aunt Gussie was chiefly irritated that her younger brother was dying first, leaving her with no one to see her out, but she comforted herself with the vindictive pleasure of saying to my grandmother, "He wants to be buried by his first wife, you know." "It's all right with me, as long as she's dead," my grandmother replied. It was Gussie who insisted on an open casket presenting a corpse no one recognized, except those few of us who had tended him in his last months. Even to me he didn't look real, simply a central prop for the ritual drama.

My grandfather Rule was on the dock to see me off on my first trip to England and dropped dead of a heart attack before I arrived. The day I heard the news, I had a date to go to Madame Tussaud's Wax Works. I went. Sleeping Beauty's mechanism was broken; she had stopped breathing. There were famous criminals wearing signs that read, "Dressed in his own clothes." Grandfather Rule had been wistful about fame, imagined founding a university which would be named after him. "Oh, beloved man," I thought, "this is all it is, to be a wax doll in this vast mausoleum."

My little grandmother had been cremated before I arrived home. My brother and I went to the funeral parlor to collect the ashes. There was no funeral. People where she lived assumed it would take place in Eureka, where her ashes were to be placed in the family mausoleum. The family there assumed it had already taken place. As we were having breakfast at the airport waiting for our flight, Mother said, "Mother never would fly. 'Over my dead body,' she said." Her ashes sat on the fourth chair at the table. If the chief mourner bids you laugh, you laugh.

At four o'clock in the morning of the day Grandmother Rule died, my mother announced, "There will be no grief," as my father talked to his sister on the phone. They did not go back for the funeral.

By now all those old people have outdied my mother's refusal to mourn them, and she remembers them quite conventionally as better than they were, more attractive, brighter, kinder, and nicer to her than they were. She doesn't speak ill of the dead. Perversely, I, who mourned each one uncertainly and in secret, remind her of their failings and tyrannies. I don't want

"My parents were nomadic..." Jane and Arthur Rule on the Galiano ferry.

the dressed-up wax effigies. I want the real people rampaging around in my imagination as they had in my life. I've never learned to let go of anyone I have loved, living or dead.

When my father was in a coma, dying, my sister offered to be the one to keep watch. "Maybe it's too hard for you, Mother." My mother looked at my sister and said, "He's mine, after all." Months after he died, my brother said to me, "Didn't he shoot you once?" He had accidentally while cleaning his shotgun. When it went off, a few pellets ricocheting off the tile floor into my thigh, Mother said in a plaintive voice, "Oh, Art, don't do that." "That proves he loved you best," my brother said.

I didn't keep watch while my father died. There was no funeral. I didn't join other members of the family who scattered his ashes on a river where he had taught us all to fish.

I sat with the image of him crawling naked down the hall of my house after a heart attack and then a stroke had felled him, an animal struggling to find a hiding place away from all the helpless witnesses to his last indignity. I was enraged that such a thing had happened to him. It was an anger so fierce it frightened me, for there was no rational place to direct it. I found myself resentful of everyone else I loved because they became for me inevitably vulnerable to similar defeats, at least some of them before my own.

"When I miss him," my mother says, "I remind myself he would be a vegetable, and I promised him I wouldn't let that happen."

When you're in your sixties before you lose a parent, something in you has learned to hope it won't have to happen. Oh, I've rarely thought I'd die before my parents did. But I must have thought they might just manage to put dying off indefinitely. Obviously what I did not do was prepare myself, learn how to grieve properly and get beyond grief to acceptance.

So I go back to those earlier family deaths to listen again to the messages I heard. Did I learn that grief is a form of vanity to be avoided at all cost or, if not avoided, certainly hidden from sight? Do not compete for a place at the bedside, for a handful of ashes. Do not weep or in any way call attention to yourself because grief isn't about the dead. It's about the living feeling sorry for themselves. Then I think grumpily, what's so morally reprehensible about feeling sorry for yourself?

My father's death was different from those other deaths. I had important relationships with all my grandparents, but they were people apart from me. In my relationship with my father there was, well hidden most of the time even from me, a child, dependent and defiant. We were often separated from my father when I was a child. Before the war he was a traveling salesman, on the road much of the time. Each summer Mother took us to her family's summer place in the redwoods where my father joined us for only two weeks of the long summer holiday. When he was with us, he was the playful, loving, teaching parent. Though lessons of most sorts were focused on my brother, I was allowed to learn, too, even the cleaning of a fish and the firing of a gun. He was the parent we wanted to please, even to impress because he pleased and impressed us, so tall, so handsome, so good at everything, a national swimming champion, a player of any musical instrument he picked up, a builder of anything from a fence to a house. His absences only more sharply defined his presence until the war came and he went away to sea for three years.

I was twelve when he left, fifteen when he came home bewildered by teenaged children who had learned to live without him and were restive under his resumed authority and his repossession of our mother. We had taken up bowling, a sport he had never tried. The first time he went with us, he beat us soundly, expecting us to be reassured by his superiority. He said of my brother's poor grades in school, "With half the effort you could do twice as well as your sister." He took me alone on a short business trip with him and said, "You know, your mother talks to me and keeps me entertained." "I guess I'm more like you," I said, and he knew it was not a compliment. We did better out fishing the river together or picking fruit, anything where our attention didn't have to be directly on each other.

I don't suppose I knew it then, but I didn't want to be under his spell again. I may have wanted to punish him for having been away those three long, hard years. I may have wanted to protect myself from needing him again.

When I left home to go away to college and to travel in Europe, my grandmother said, "You're breaking your father's heart." "He was gone for three years," I said, "and I coped. It's his turn now."

He tried to take an interest in things that interested me. When I was home from college talking about being a writer, he decided he should show me how to write a story that would sell. He wrote one and asked which was the highest paying magazine. "The *Ladies' Home Journal*," I told him. The story came back with a rejection slip, the best confirmation I could have that my choice of career was the right one for me. He said wistfully, "You're now climbing trees too high for me to get you down." "You've taught me to do it for myself." But what had really taught me was his absence. Did I never forgive him for it? Was some part of me left in a tree I couldn't get down from without him?

Because I didn't marry, he didn't give me away as he did his younger daughter. It was agreeable to him if I wanted to live at home and write, but, if I wanted to be independent, I must earn my own way. It seemed a more reasonable expectation to me than it did to him who was never really comfortable about my providing for myself. For the first several years he sent me a small allowance which he could ill afford. He came to visit with expensive gifts, hi-fi sets, typewriters. He built cupboards, bookshelves, wine racks, finally several rooms in the house I live in now. He was in his seventies by then, still swimming in the Masters program, assuring that his team stayed first in the nation.

He wouldn't swim in the pool I had put in. Was it too small in comparison to the public pools he was used to? "He was funny about some things," my mother says. I think it felt unseemly to him that I should have provided such an extravagance for myself. He played my hi-fi which wasn't as fine as his, but he'd given it to me.

Before they made their last visit, my father had set the destination as something to get well enough to do. "I'll sit on the deck and swim in the pool." He did both. And then he died.

"He did what he set out to do," people said. "He won his last race."

My father was a kind and generous man to many people. He was a kind and generous father to all his children, forgiving us our failures, accepting what he couldn't easily understand. Perhaps for him taking that final swim, old champion in his daughter's small pool, was an act of humility he thought he owed me or I wanted.

I've been perching in this tree of raging grief ever since. "Face it, sweetie," my father said to me once when I complained about unequal salaries for women at the university, "it's a man's world." "I will not!" I retorted. "I'll change it." His laugh rang out surprised and at the same time recognizing the will in me he'd had to contend with since I was a small child.

I sulk and mutter, surrounded by his gifts, not just the bookcases and the very walls of my study but such silly things as a wind-up Victrola to have music even in a power failure. He gave me that when I stubbornly refused to put in a generator he would have provided.

If I never quite managed to forgive him for going away to war, how on earth am I going to learn to forgive him for dying? Thinking I have to is, I suppose, another way of refusing his death. But what a horrible example he has set for everyone else I love!

It's the tree of life I'm in, Father, Sir, Dad, and you don't get me down, and I don't get myself down either. I fall, after you.

# A HOLE IN THE GROUND

{ September 2007 }

I have grown accustomed to the fact that things outlast people. In singular old age I sit in the chair of a grandmother and wear her rings, surrounded by walls raised by my father, over my knees an afghan my mother knitted, wearing my lover's shirt. I try to take comfort in, rather than resent, the survival of things beyond the fragile, transient flesh of those I have loved.

I am therefore startled and then bewildered to discover that my twenty-eight-year-old swimming pool has developed a leak which cannot be mended in an irreplaceable liner. For days I top up the pool with a limited supply of well water before I admit defeat, turn off the pump and daily watch the water level go down until there is only about a foot of increasingly green water in the bottom of the pool.

This is the first summer I am too arthritic to swim in it myself. The principal reason we built the pool was for me to postpone as long as possible the immobility of the disease which was diagnosed when I was forty-five, with the prediction that I would be in a wheelchair within five years. I put off that chair for nearly thirty years, chiefly by swimming.

It seemed to me at the time an alarming extravagance. I tried at first to suggest contributing generously to the building of a community pool, but, on this little island of only a thousand residents, there were neither enough people interested in swimming nor the community spirit to undertake such a project. So we built a modest pool in our own backyard, forty feet by twelve feet by four and a half.

My father, who had owned a pool in his retirement, warned against it, particularly in a community where there were no professional pool-tenders. It took only half an hour a week to clean it, but the water chemistry had to be checked daily to avoid invasions of algae, and it was not safe to leave swimmers unattended. In trouble, a pool can be as demanding as an invalid or a child. But, loving island summers and free to travel at other times of the year, we didn't think we would mind the demands of a pool. In the ordinary course of events, we didn't. There was an occasional emergency, an exploding propane heater, a child falling into the mint bed, but we switched to solar panels and a heat pump, had better railings built.

It was a new kind of swimming for me. I had learned to swim in a river, remember the day, when I was about four, that my father took off my rubber ring, saying it was getting in the way, and I swam off. My brother and I swam for fun, for the diving for rocks, the chasing of fish, riding the currents. We swam as a way to travel the river, cross it, go upstream or down. I was bewildered in the city to swim in pools, not only because they were limited and crowded, but because we were expected to race, to beat other people. Now, in our little pool, I learned to swim lengths, to increase my stamina, until I was swimming a mile a day.

Aside from our house guests, other adults also swam for exercise, for health, for pleasure. Those who wanted had set times to use the pool. I watched people recover from strokes, hip surgery, broken bones. Occasionally an adult, phobic about water, asked to be taught to swim.

But the children of the island were my chief concern. Nearly none of them knew how to swim, the ocean too cold and rough for learning. I life-guarded from three to five in the afternoon, seven days a week. At first I thought of the job as nothing more than ensuring their safety, teaching them not to run on the deck, push each other in, duck each other. But soon I realized they also needed to be taught co-operation and civility if they were going to enjoy themselves and I was going to enjoy them. Island children are clannish, unwelcoming to strangers, inclined to exclude or taunt children they don't know. And on fractious afternoons they could stoop to tormenting each other. So I made rules about the treatment of strangers, rules against games which were simply excuses to bully or cast out. Teaching them also to test the chemistry of the pool, to tidy their toys before they left, made the pool more their own.

"The children of the island were my chief concern."

As I grew too old and disabled for such work, we limited the children's use of the pool to a couple of afternoons a week, with more parental involvement. In the last few years I've begun to watch the children of my first children learn to swim here.

It's been eight years since Helen took her last swim in the pool. She was suffering from lack of balance, had fallen and hurt herself so that she hadn't been able to swim for some time. She was also beginning to lose her memory. I watched her take her first tentative steps into the water and then, as she went under, I realized she'd forgotten how to swim. I pulled her to the side steps and helped her out of the water. I watched my father, too, still with a swimmer's body and eighty-eight years old, take his last swim. He died of a stroke and heart attack a week later.

I didn't know it was my last swim at the end of last summer. It was difficult for me to get to the pool, but I had a walker on the deck and flat stones to make the steps easier for me. I was still swimming fifty lengths a day. I couldn't kick but my arms were still strong, and I was free in the water to move without clinging to anything, without fear of falling.

I often remembered then teaching handicapped children to swim, a job I had when I was in college. There was a ramp for wheelchairs to be taken right into the pool, where we could remove the sandbags which held in place children with cerebral palsy and polio. Gradually those children learned to move in the water, some of them physically free and independent for the first time in their lives.

The liner has been removed from the pool. A few planks have been pried up from the deck by people who can use the wood. The main job of getting rid of it is still to be done. I'm not yet quite sure how. There are solar panels, pumps and heaters, the steel pool-shell, the chemicals and cleaning equipment, as well as the large deck and dressing rooms. The process may take months and be costly. I hope at least some of the things can be recycled. Until it is done, I have to look out on what was once a pretty sight of clear blue water, often filled with children who now miss it more than I do.

It is appropriate to mourn the death of a person, even of a pet. And we easily understand the shock at the loss of a house to fire, earthquake, flood, among the many things, important or not, that should outlive us. But a pool? It's just a hole in the ground with water in it, a status symbol, an expense, a nuisance. Why does it seem to me so much like an open grave?

## ACCIDENTAL ODDS

{ December 2005 }

Months ago I noticed a bubble on the upper broiling element of the oven. I only thought of it when I was about to fix dinner for friends and found myself wondering if this would be the evening it finally burst or burned out, whatever a bubble might be promising to do, in the same way I often fruitlessly wonder about power failures when a turkey is in the oven. Finally it occurred to me that I didn't really have to wait passively for the catastrophe. I called a repair man and had the element replaced.

It should be easier than it apparently is to sort out what accidents waiting to happen can be averted and what are out of the reach of control. "If it ain't broke, don't fix it," appeals both to my defense against useless anxiety and my lazy fatalism.

Old age is an accident waiting to happen. Some of us are quick to phone the repair man at the first sign of trouble, a twinge in the gut, a pain in the arm, a moment of vertigo. Through diet, medication, exercise and surgery, we coax the failing body into detours on the mortal road, even if the surface is rougher or the scenery turns ugly. Others of us ignore the signs, refuse the remedies and simply continue to falter down the decline to whatever the end is. But most of us oscillate between those extremes, trying to be realistic and moderate in our hope for medical aid. If we can't improve our bodies, we try to improve our circumstances: get rid of the scatter rugs, raise chairs and toilet seats, swap cane for walker, agree to some home help. Most of us put off the decision to move into real assisted living, hoping sudden death will eliminate the problem. It is more likely a broken hip or Alzheimer's will take the decision out of our hands and leave our relatives or the local authorities to find solutions.

It is a puzzle to me that babies, who are incontinent, unable to feed themselves or walk or speak, are so cherished when old people with the same limitations are put away in care out of sight. Well, I think, babies get better. Old people don't, nor, however, do they go on forever, though some seem to. If there were the same sort of timetable for the old that there is for the young, would all of us know better how to cope?

If I could know how much longer I'd be able to wash my own hair, remember to turn off the stove, balance my checkbook, it would be easier to make decisions. Some people do pack themselves off to assisted living while they are still capable of making the decision and even find relief from loneliness, from anxiety, from the increasing difficulty of managing daily life. But for far too many others it is a plunge into loneliness, anxiety and defeat.

"But everyone here is so old!" my sister-in-law cries, and tries to figure out how to move back into her admittedly too large house.

"My children don't like to visit here. They find it depressing."

In the senior citizen complex my parents moved into, wheelchairs and walkers were not allowed in the main dining room for fear of putting off guests. Those who couldn't manage ate in their rooms or in the infirmary dining room on the second floor.

I have heard hospital staff joke about special insurance for those assigned to care for the old who, even if they are helpless to clean and feed themselves, can turn abusive and even violent. I saw one patient on an orthopedic ward throw her breakfast tray at a nurse whose own impatience and bad temper were a trial to everyone on the ward. My sympathy was entirely for the patient. But caring for the helpless and angry old is not an easy job. The temptation to abuse is very like the temptation to abuse wilful and unruly children. But the old are often more isolated and therefore less protected.

If I knew that I was in the last weeks of my life, I'd rather be in a hospital, cared for by professionals, than be a burden to inexperienced people whose very caring for me would make caring for me more difficult. Dying in hospital is just fine, but living in one is a different matter. And who can know that odd shift when dying extends into living?

What is under my control? What can be fixed? Though my eye no longer is much troubled by worn carpets, stained furniture, chipped china, these things are still subject to my will. There is virtue in cleaning, mending, or throwing away, a surprisingly new virtue to me of "keeping up appearances." Perhaps preparing to die is really about going on living, just a little more against the odds than it used to be. It is early December. The Christmas presents are all wrapped. The freezer is full of food. I may or may not be here, but I'm ready. So is the stove.

ACKNOWLEDGEMENTS

The following essays in this collection
were previously published:

"Deception[s] in Search of the Truth." *Language in
Her Eye: Views on Writing and Gender by Canadian Women
Writing in English*. Ed. Libby Scheier, Sarah Sheard
and Eleanor Wachtel (Toronto, 1990)

"You be Normal or Else...."
*Resources for Feminist Research*, 19 (1991)

"Mills, 1948–1952" as "Tolerance: It Isn't Polite Silence."
*Mills Quarterly* 75.1 (July, 1992)

"Choosing Home." *Writing Home: A PEN Anthology*,
ed. Constance Rooke (Toronto, 1997)

"I Want to Speak Ill of the Dead." *Brick* 58 (Winter, 1998)

"Grief." *Go Big* 3 (2001)

"Labels." *BC BookWorld* 19.1 (Spring, 2005)

"Our Mothers" as "A Tribute to our Literary Mothers."
*Herizons* 19.4 (Spring, 2006)

———

Thanks to Alison, Ali,
Shelagh, Gwen and Kendall.

Born in Plainfield, New Jersey in 1931, Jane Vance Rule
received her B.A. from Mills College, California and taught
for two years at Concord Academy, Massachusetts, where she
met Helen Sonthoff with whom she lived from 1956 until Helen's
death in 2000. After twenty years of working periodically at the
University of British Columbia, she moved to Galiano Island,
where she became a much-loved and generous contributor to
the island community. She died at her Galiano home in
November, 2007.

Jane Rule's seven novels present a range of characters in
a variety of situations but it is for her unapologetic and clear-
eyed writing on lesbian themes that she is best known. Her
first published novel, *Desert of the Heart*, became a classic of
lesbian literature; it was made into the film *Desert Hearts*.
Her commissioned book *Lesbian Images* is a pioneering study
of the often veiled forms in which women have written of love
between women. She was also a prolific writer of short stories
and essays, published in four previous collections. For ten years
she wrote a column headed "So's your Grandmother" for the
gay liberationist newspaper *The Body Politic*.

Jane Rule's account of her own life was published in the
Gage autobiography series *Contemporary Authors* (18) and she
appears in the award-winning film about her life and work
entitled *Fiction and Other Truths*. Marilyn Schuster's scholarly
study is entitled *Passionate Communities: Reading Lesbian
Resistance in Jane Rule's Fiction*.

The recipient of numerous awards in recognition of her work
as writer and social activist, Jane Rule was inducted into the Order
of British Columbia in 1998 and the Order of Canada in 2007.